The Art Of Aging Joyfully

DARYL V. HOOLE

Grandma Moses @Everett Collection Historical / Alamy Stock Photo. Used with permission.

She will find what is lost, ©Brian T. Kershisnik, 2012. Used with permission.

Published in the United States by Books to Hook Publishing, LLC.

Hardback: 978-1-962071-16-1

Paperback: 978-1-962071-17-8
Ebook: 978-1-962071-18-5
Audiobook: 978-1-962071-19-2

Printed in the United States of America.

10 9 8 7 6 5 4 3 2

First Edition

darylhoole.com

COVER PIECE

In contemplating a cover design, I chose the swallow, a beautiful songbird. It represents positivity, joy, hope, and good luck. I wanted it to be soaring through the air which feels very free, happy, and joyful to me. I also love the spiritual symbolism of such a bird—peace, love, eternity.

--Angie Panian, graphic artist, designer

Table of Contents

Preface

The year is 2023, and family members and friends have underscored a feeling I have had for some time which is to write—again. It was in 1962 that my first book, *The Art of Homemaking*, was published. Now some of these supporters are reading my mind by suggesting another book: *The Art of Aging Joyfully.* Their interest, encouragement, and contributions have been a motivating force behind this effort.

I was 28 years old when I wrote that first book. The next 40 years found me busily engaged in writing and speaking publicly about home management and family living.

This was in addition to raising our eight living children and serving in the Church of Jesus Christ of Latter-day Saints, which included ward, stake, and general callings. The efforts were mutually connected, one seeming to support and strengthen the other. To further explain, I was more successful in one area because of the other and vice versa. It was a highly fulfilling time in my life.

During the next 20 or so years, Hank and I, in our sixties and seventies, enjoyed some discretionary time which we devoted to lots of grandparenting and some traveling. We also accepted two mission calls, one to the Netherlands where we served as mission leaders for three years and the other to Hong Kong where we served as Asia Area welfare/humanitarian administrators along with two other couples for two years.

Hank's health began to fail as he turned eighty and I became his caregiver, which was a labor of love. He passed away in 2013 at age 83 from complications of Parkinson's Disease.

Now, in my 90th year, I am still writing (mostly in my journal), speaking (albeit informally to my friends and associates), and I continue to be deeply involved with my large family (except now they help me), and my focus has evolved. My challenges this time are about aging, being a widow, living alone, and making the most of every opportunity to express love and gratitude to my 8 children, 36 grandchildren, and 68 (and counting) great-grandchildren.

This book is written with those challenges in mind, an eternal perspective, and a divinely determined purpose in life due to my dedication to the Church. Every chapter reflects my faith in the gospel of Jesus Christ. This faith makes *the* difference in my attitude, actions, decisions, desires, and prayers—all that I am and all that I do and all that I hope to become.

This eternal focus has become paramount in my thinking as my life on this earth enters another decade. Central to *everything* are keeping commandments, honoring covenants, and cherishing relationships with our families, others, and the Lord. Worldly pursuits are only for sustaining life, not consuming it. My efforts revolve around that which will clear celestial customs someday.

Even though you, as my friends and readers, may have circumstances and life situations that are vastly different in many significant ways, I believe we are all very much the same in what matters most.

Each of us desires to be physically and mentally healthy, self-reliant, and as fulfilled as possible. We want to feel loved, accepted, and needed. We would like this season of our time on earth to be a rewarding one. We want life— and we hope for it abundantly. This comes to us best by way of daily walking the covenant path. We are sustained in doing so by family, friends, and faith in Jesus Christ.

It is with Jesus Christ that we, you and I, have the covenant relationship. And it is only through Jesus Christ and completely through Jesus Christ and always through Jesus Christ that joy is ours.

May this be foremost in your thinking on every page as you read this book.

–Daryl

CHAPTER ONE

Being Of Good Cheer

Years ago, as I was preparing material for a home management class I would be teaching on attitude, I turned to the scriptures to see how many times the word "attitude" appeared. To my astonishment, it was not listed. Not once. Instead, however, I found numerous references to the phrase, "Be of good cheer."

Not only was "being of good cheer" cited as a virtue in each instance; it was defined as a commandment, even by the Lord himself.

We are admonished to go forth with good cheer. We are living in a time when we will see things both wonderful and terrible. There is no way that we can be part of the last days and have it otherwise. Nevertheless, the Lord commands us to be of good cheer.

Jesus Christ has given that same instruction to others before, when the stressful circumstances in which they found themselves were anything but cheerful. For instance, He told the original Twelve to be of good cheer when, on the surface, there was nothing to be cheerful about. The indescribable agonies of Gethsemane were imminent. Then would come the final, awful hours on Calvary.

How could the Savior expect the Twelve to be of good cheer? Because, the Savior explained, "In the world ye shall have tribulation, but be of good cheer; I have overcome the world" (John 16:33). Because Christ overcame the world, Satan's effort to frustrate the plan of salvation was vanquished. Moreover, not only may we overcome sin and death through Christ's Atonement, but we may receive the Lord's healing succor in the face of life's adversities (Alma 7:11-12). Truly there is much about which to be of good cheer.

Elder Neal A. Maxwell reminded us: "Being of good cheer is part of being valiant in the testimony of Jesus. . . . In those moments when we feel the pain which is a necessary part of the Great Plan of Happiness, we can remember that there was an ancient time when that plan was first unveiled. Then the perceptive among us voted not secretly, but audibly—by shouting for joy! Let us not go back on those feelings now—for we saw more clearly then what we are experiencing now!" ("Be of Good Cheer," General Conference, October 1982).

In my memory's eye, I can still see Elder Maxwell, one of the greatest speakers and most quoted of all general authorities, at the pulpit explaining the plan of salvation in his profoundly insightful way. I loved to hear him speak, and I took advantage, with note pad in hand, to hear him talk at every opportunity.

Elder Boyd K. Packer also immortalized many of his teachings by painting pictures with words. Years ago, I recall his teaching us about the plan of salvation by comparing it to a three-act play. "Mortality is the second act," he explained, and "living happily thereafter is reserved for the third act, if during this life, we endure to the end in good cheer" ("The Play and the Plan," *CES Fireside*, 7 May 1995, Kirkland, WA).

I value the gospel concept of being of good cheer. I appreciate studying about it through our leaders' talks, lessons, and the holy scriptures.

Cheerfulness is a condition, more of the mind than of circumstance, and it is worthy of cultivation. I seek association with cheerful people. I thrive in a cheerful environment. I am gladdened by things that are sunny and bright.

I love the color yellow. To me, the sunflower is a wonderful symbol of good cheer. I am happy it blooms prolifically in the hills, along the roadsides, and in our gardens. Sunflowers are a delight to see: In the morning, all the sunflowers face east and by late afternoon their heads are turned west. They follow the sun.

There are trials that test us and lessons to be learned in every phase of the world and in each stage of life. Growing older presents its own unique way to determine our individual level of good cheer.

Certainly, as we age, it seems that the temperature, so to speak, has been turned up. The increased heat polishes many of us into fine steel. Some others are burned by the heat.

During this especially challenging time of life, I find it helpful to put forth extra effort and a keen awareness, if necessary, to avoid murmuring and complaining. It is likewise a kindness to others not to become grumpy, irritable, or difficult to live with.

Even though frustrations, limitations, and pain mount, so does the chance to be cheerful expand. Many people mellow with age and grow kinder and gentler.

What better way to respond to a spouse or other family member or caregiver than with a smile on your face and gladness in your heart. I know this to be true from personal experience. My husband, as a Parkinson's disease sufferer, was consistently pleasant, cooperative, and appreciative of my help. For me it was sweet service—a privilege and blessing —to serve and care for him during the three years before he passed.

Happily, there are many among us who are doing their best to be of good cheer despite their aches and pains and problems.

Please meet my close neighbor, fellow ward member, and very good friend, Jackie Gardner. I have enjoyed her association immensely through six decades of treasured friendship as adults. Now another dimension to our relationship is being added as we are both widows and living alone, and she faces serious age-related physical health problems.

She is experiencing increasingly diminishing eyesight as the effects of macular degeneration manifest themselves every day. The distressing symptoms of Parkinson's disease steadily advance. Almost beyond endurance back pain causes agony with every step. Yet she smiles and pushes onward.

I would suppose that sometimes during private, quiet moments of the day she shakes her fist in the air and sheds some tears in her pillow at night as she anguishes and admits to herself how hard life can be, but then she braces herself and courageously gets up and presses forward. She is showing me and others how to be of good cheer regardless of aging problems. Just like old times, she greets everyone she meets with a lilt in her voice, a smile on her face, and something positive to say about the day.

As an older adult, I want to remember always that He who knows the path perfectly has promised: "Be of good cheer, for I will lead you along. The kingdom is yours . . . and the riches of eternity" (Doctrine and Covenants 78:18).

Our Savior has asked us to be of good cheer, and He is there to help us do just that. Let us be like the sunflower and follow the Son each day.

Recipe for a Cheerful Day

Get up

Dress up

Show up

CHAPTER TWO

Giving Thanks In All Things

It was a cold, bleak wintry day, and I woke up to snow covering the ground. I gave thanks to God. The snow was an answer to prayer—many prayers.

Utah and the surrounding western states were experiencing a severe drought. One snowstorm does not solve the water problem, but every storm does help, and this winter of 2022-23 had been a snowy one. Many Utah citizens had been praying for rain, and we were grateful for the precipitation.

One of the compensations of old age and widowhood for me is lots of quiet time to think and ponder. I took advantage of it early that snowy morning. My house was quiet and still, so I rolled over in bed for a few extra winks. As I did so, my mind turned to giving thanks for the snow in connection with a medical report I had recently read, which stated:

> "In positive psychology research, gratitude is strongly and consistently associated with greater happiness. Gratitude helps people feel more positive emotions, relish good health, deal with adversity, and build strong relationships" ("Giving thanks can make you happier," *Harvard Health Publishing*, August 2021).

Furthermore, I recalled Janice Kaplan in her book, *The Gratitude Diaries*, writing that gratitude aids all body systems in their function.

As I've aged, I have become aware of gaining a well-earned perspective that I didn't have as a younger person. I see things I may have missed before.

For instance, maturity has made me grateful for health, where I may have taken it for granted in my youth. I'm grateful for the medications that I take, which I feel were inspired from God. I am grateful for a simple and ordinary day, a loyal friend, a caring family member, a spectacular sunset, or a thoughtful act of kindness.

That morning while getting ready for the day, I could hear metal scraping against concrete, and I realized my strong, kind neighbors, Marty, and his teenage son Henry, were clearing the snow from the walks and driveway. They are busy with work, school, and sports, so their sacrifice of time and effort meant a lot to me. I opened the door and called out an enthusiastic "thank you" to them.

The phone rang a few times during the morning, and I chatted with family members and friends, something I thoroughly enjoy. I spent a rewarding hour or so emailing and texting, thankful for such a blessed connection with more of my favorite people. I am profoundly grateful for these relationships, many of them lifelong, all of them hopefully everlasting.

It was a Tuesday, so at 11:00 AM I turned my TV on to listen to the weekly BYU devotional. I am thankful that I have the time to listen to inspired leaders and other outstanding speakers who bring great messages to me in my own home.

Early in the afternoon there was a noise at my front door, and I knew our letter carrier, Joe, had just delivered the mail. Joe is more than an average mailman. If a package is to be delivered, he rings the doorbell. If I'm not home, he takes the package to the back door as a convenience to me and to keep it safe. This reminded me of something that took place a few days after my husband Hank passed away in 2013. Joe rang the doorbell to offer condolences regarding his death. Joe had noted a lot of cars parked at the ward building and inquired about a funeral. His brief visit to me was a surprising but appreciated expression of sympathy.

I then spent several hours with the scriptures and my *"Come, Follow Me"* study guide. I also listened to a podcast by Latter-day Saint religion scholars representing *Scripture Central*. I am grateful they share their extensive knowledge with me; it's like attending an Institute of Religion class every day.

The doorbell rang around 5:00 in the afternoon. It was my ministering brothers bringing me a message and an offer "to do anything to be of service." I felt grateful to them and was reminded of my ministering sisters who also drop by often with kind words and thoughtful deeds. I eagerly anticipate their visits. (See Chapter 13)

For dinner I warmed fine food a loving daughter Jean had "plated" for me from their Sunday dinner. It tasted so good. I get these delicious dinners often. I am very grateful to Jean and to each woman in my family for their life-sustaining generosity. True, it really is lifesaving. I've pretty much closed my kitchen because, as an "oldie," it seems I drop or spill everything I touch. If eating were left up to me, I'm afraid I would survive on just cheese and crackers. (Not really, but I did appreciate the food.)

Then, because I have only myself to please—living alone means it is my privilege to do all the choosing—I decided to relax and complete the day with a favorite movie on my TV. Thank you, technology!

> I feel like the elderly gentleman who explained:
>
> "I'm drinkin' from my saucer, 'cause my cup is overflowed."
>
> —Unknown

The happenings of the day are mostly just the little things. Yet, they point clearly to the bigger blessings of mortal life such as health, means, family, friends, purpose, home, and happiness.

Above all are the priceless, everlasting blessings of being a daughter of God, of having a testimony of the restored gospel of Jesus Christ, of being part of a covenant relationship with Jesus Christ, of having the God-given promise of an eternal family, and of being sealed to a wonderful, worthy eternal companion. I rejoice!

A thankful heart can be cultivated by being aware of all things to be grateful for each day. The more you see and acknowledge, the more there will be to see and acknowledge.

Giving thanks to God is essential to our spiritual well-being. The word of God as recorded in the Doctrine and Covenants is a scripture to live by. It states:

> "Verily I say unto you my friends, fear not, let your hearts be comforted; yea, rejoice evermore, and in everything give thanks." (Doctrine and Covenants 98:1).

> Acknowledging God's hand in our lives helps us to have humility, and it protects us from pride. Also, commandments have temporal as well as spiritual blessings. Giving thanks in all things helps us to have a perspective that will enhance every aspect of our lives.

On my way through the house to my bedroom, joy was mine as I passed a whiteboard where grandchildren had written words of appreciation in the language of their mission.

It had been a good day: interesting, impressive, and insightful. I summed up a l-o-n-g list of "thank-yous" to my Father in Heaven in my bedtime prayer. I felt a sense of peace. . . Then I went to sleep counting my blessings.

Thank you notes from my grandchildren in their mission languages

CHAPTER THREE

Living Graciously In Every Situation

"Finishing School"—perhaps you have heard about it. Generally speaking, finishing school was an institution from a time gone by to educate young women, usually from wealthy families, in social graces. It was fine training in deportment and etiquette. It was about being polite and saying "please" and "thank you," and modeling other social graces. Summed up, it was all the above plus lessons on such personal refinements as which fork to use at the dinner table.

My sister, Donette, and I never attended a finishing school, but our mother did create a home-school "curriculum" that went well beyond "please" and "thank you" and forks. It was a required "class" for my two brothers, as well. She made certain that "How can I help?" and "I am sorry" were also on the list. In the event of conflict, she taught us that the nicest one would apologize first. She endeavored to make our home a practice field for developing lifetime habits that could enhance our lives and enrich others' lives through graciousness.

Our mother thoughtfully pointed out the benefits of tempering these virtues with cultural norms, moderation, flexibility, and spontaneity—even humor. It was okay to laugh at ourselves.

Over the years, I've noted there are variations and exceptions to these "rules," and there is often more than one way to say or do something right, but for the most part Mother's teachings were reliable.

I've also observed there are levels or degrees of graciousness, such as "thank you" and "THANK YOU." For instance, one time I bought an expensive airline ticket for someone in need. She responded with a polite "thank you." Several weeks later I received a phone call from her. She was at the airport, boarding the flight, and thanked me once again by saying with deep feeling that she wouldn't be making this important trip were it not for the gift of the ticket. This additional call was "THANK YOU."

The following story, a favorite of mine, shows graciousness in action:

> After World War II, Queen Juliana of the Netherlands hosted a lavish dinner at the royal palace for farmers from a northern province in the country. The purpose for this occasion was to officially honor and thank these men for averting starvation among the Dutch people during the war because of the vast amounts of potatoes they grew and harvested.
>
> This was a grand affair with the fanciest in food and finery, including a finger bowl at each place around the table. These unschooled farmers had never seen finger bowls and didn't know what to do with them, so they drank the water. Not to embarrass them, the queen drank from her finger bowl, too.
>
> Queen Juliana, a beloved monarch, was known for her graciousness and humanity. She did not just do gracious things, she was gracious. She endeavored to do the right things for the right reason.

Graciousness knows no age—19 or 90. Rules apply regardless of the years. Social graces are always noted and appreciated. A gentleman is still a gentleman, a lady is still a lady.

There is another facet of graciousness that is sometimes forgotten in this chaotic and often confusing world. It is that we, even at advancing age, would do well to take more thought and time in communicating with one another kindly, politely, and effectively. This means we should not be critical or judgmental of others. It is considerate to return missed telephone calls promptly, respond as soon as possible to messages, follow through with our promises and obligations, and respond to R.S.V.P. requests. It is the gracious thing to do.

When you grow older and become slower, you can still be a reliable communicator, even if you have to keep notes on yourself. It is the gracious thing to do.

Something else of particular significance to those of us who are getting closer to 100 than we are to 50: There comes a time when, if we are gracious, we will relinquish the leadership and responsibility in our family and pass the "baton" on. A friend pointed this out when she introduced a book to me titled, *Let Evening Come. . . Reflections on Aging* by Mary C. Morris. She said one of the most helpful things she gathered from the book was "how to gracefully move to the periphery of life and pass being the center of activity to the next generation." It is the gracious thing to do.

An excerpt from the book reads: "It is time to give up the old habit of being in control, of deciding what is to be done or not done. This is difficult. We have spent the best years of our lives learning the managerial skills that family life demands. . . How can we possibly lay them down? But now we must do so, and as gracefully as possible" (Mary C. Morris, *Let Evening Come... Reflections on Aging*).

We hope for a world where *all* people are civil and kind in *all* situations and circumstances. It sounds like heaven on earth. I believe that is what the Millennium will be like when Christ comes back to earth to reign.

Graciousness is much more than an act; it is a way of life. It is a character trait. It is something that can grow and develop deeply within us over the years. As a person, it can become who we are: gracious. It is the way to be.

It is the Golden Rule. I like the wording by which Jesus Christ taught this:

> "Therefore, all things whatsoever ye would that men should do to you, do ye even so to them, for this is the law and the prophets" (3 Nephi 14:12).

With or without a finishing school degree, being gracious gets high marks.

CHAPTER FOUR

Creating Your Own Little World At Home

"Home is where you hang your heart!" someone said. True. I love my home. Next to being in the temple, I am happiest at home. My home is the center of my universe; it's my world. I have lived in this same house for sixty years, excluding missions. During some of those years, there were ten of us here (Hank and I and our eight living children). I cherish the memories. Now it is just me. I am home alone. But the walls "talk" and I relish in memories from busy, happy by-gone times.

My Home, a Comforting Place to Be

My home has always functioned well for me. I have taken good care of it, keeping the inside clean and tidy and the outside well-maintained. I love to sit at my desk and watch families walk by on their way to the nearby park or to look out my kitchen window and enjoy the flowers, birds, and trees in my backyard. I find joy in being surrounded by family photos, pictures, and mementos from missions and special places I have visited with Hank and our family.

A few years ago, I decided to begin disposing of the things that no longer served me. Ever since I was a young woman, I maintained files of articles, talks, and other important information. I helped many people learn how to "file and find it again." However, in the digital age, my files became obsolete. Most of the information I had stored in large files in my office could now easily be found with a quick google search. And so, I squared my shoulders, took a deep breath, and emptied my filing cabinets. While I was at it, I also discarded financial records that were no longer necessary to keep. Even many books were donated to those who would enjoy them.

I recently became aware of the concept of Döstädning, or Swedish Death Cleaning. In her book, *The Gentle Art of Swedish Death Cleaning*, the author, Margareta Magnussen, says, "Whether it's sorting the family heirlooms from the junk, downsizing to a smaller place, or setting up a system to help you stop misplacing your keys, death cleaning gives us the chance to make the later years of our lives as comfortable and stress-free as possible."

Actually, this is what I have been doing over the years. My latest project was to have all our home videos digitized and given to my children for Christmas. Before that, Hank and I digitized our family photos as part of writing our life stories. My children have commented on how they are relieved they won't have to deal with boxes and boxes of papers when I am gone.

My Home, a Gathering Place

I love people. I love having them in my home—the welcome mat is always out for family, friends, and neighbors. The sound of the doorbell ringing at the front door or someone working the lock box at the backdoor delights me. I am eager to receive visitors.

In days past, I enjoyed hosting family dinners and having friends come and join me over a good meal, but the days of entertaining guests with big dinners, barbecues, and parties have given way to the snack tray. The snack tray isn't too bad, however, because I am able, at my advanced age, to keep it stocked and available, and new traditions are building around it.

 It's really quite simple—just a large tray that can be used inside or outside and upon which "goodies" are placed along with napkins and drinking cups. Little jars with decorative lids (jam containers from the grocery store) can hold such treats as chocolate nuggets, M&Ms, cinnamon bears, fruit snacks, fun size candy bars, and salted cashew nuts.

If you have grandchildren, by all means reserve a box, or a shelf, or a closet, or even a room for toys and games. We had a spare room that we turned into a  "Grandma Room" where toys that have been loved by two generations of children are being played with again. It has become such a big attraction in the family that little ones run to it squealing with excitement as they enter my house. When it's time to leave, they often cling to the door frame  as they cry and beg to stay. Such a response can really give Oma's ego a boost! (By the way, to simplify things, I am "Oma" to the great-grandchildren.)

My Home, a Refuge, a Safe Place

There are women of all ages who sometimes feel bored at home. The work seems monotonous, the doorbell doesn't ring, and the phone is silent. That's when it is time to get creative and not let those feelings get the best of them.

They need a project. How about setting up a "toolbox" as a reservoir of ideas for projects? It can be done in two steps:

First, select a small, empty container and label it "TOOL-BOX." You can decorate it a bit or just leave it plain.

Second, fill it with items (tools) for "fixing" your boredom and/or loneliness, such as lists of the following:

- Friends to call for a phone chat
- Friends to invite over or to go see
- Birthday greetings and thank you notes
- Books to read
- Articles, talks, etc. to read
- Things to write—your journal or life story
- Movies to see

- Programs or podcasts to watch

- Keepsakes for great-grandchildren to treasure

- Music for listening or for playing the piano, guitar, ukulele, etc.

- People in need of attention and/or care— for ministering and service

- Projects or repair jobs about your house or yard—for your attention

Christmas stockings skillfully knitted by daughter, Rebecca

- Recipes for a cooking spree in the kitchen

- Cookies to bake and share

- Ideas for a hobby such as quilting, ceramics, wood carving, or painting pictures

- Ideas for composing poems and/or essays

- Patterns and materials for handwork such as knitting and crocheting, and other craft projects

- Pictures, mementoes, and other items that trigger positive memories in your life

- Exercises and/or outdoor activities
- Games to play

Some things that won't "fit" into a toolbox, but could also be helpful are:

- Get a pet
- Raise a vegetable garden or cultivate a flower bed—even one plant or flower in a pot can be rewarding
- Become the neighborhood handyman

This "toolbox" concept is shared with compliments of my daughter, Elaine H. Quinn. As a mental health coach, Elaine used these tools in working with clients. She gives greater detail in her book *IT'S TIME--Living a Full and Joyful Life with Depression and Anxiety,* available through Amazon and Barnes and Noble. (See also Chapter 7)

My Home, A Sanctuary, A Consecrated Place

Above all, and most important to me, is to arrange my life and manage my home so it becomes a sanctuary, a holy place. In the last few years, I haven't been able to attend the temple as often as I would like, so I'm grateful that my home can be a sacred space for me. Bishop Gérald Caussé, of the Presiding Bishopric, said, "Our homes are sacred places where the Spirit can abound—as much as, and sometimes even more than in our formal places of worship." It is my desire that anyone who enters my home can feel the spirit here. President Russell M. Nelson, our prophet, promises this will happen when we strive to remember and act upon the following conditions and invitations:

- The language of love is spoken there.
- The guiding, directing, comforting, and constant influence of the Holy Ghost is present.
- The covenant path passes through it.
- Personal revelation is received.
- The Sabbath is a delight.
- The Spirit permeates every room.
- Those who live there:
    - Are peacemakers.
    - Avoid personal conflict.
    - Forgive others, including themselves.
    - Cultivate a desire to overcome the world.
    - Let God prevail in their lives.

These are the latter days and much of the world is in turmoil. There is vast suffering among mankind. Chaos and confusion prevail. Corruption is rampant in high places, including many governments. There is overall discouragement, even fear and despair in countless instances. I am grateful that my own, personal little world—my home—can be filled with love, light, truth, peace, and joy.

CHAPTER FIVE

Preparing Wisely For Life's Happenings

The Parable of the Ten Virgins is timeless. It, like each of the Savior's parables, is as relevant today as it was two thousand years ago when Jesus taught it to his followers in the Holy Land. Actually, its message of being prepared is increasing in significance as the Second Coming of the Savior draws nearer.

This powerful parable in the book of Matthew of the New Testament reads:

"Then shall the kingdom of heaven be likened unto ten virgins, which took their lamps, and went forth to meet the bridegroom.

"And five of them were wise, and five were foolish.

"They that were foolish took their lamps, and took no oil with them:

"But the wise took oil in their vessels with their lamps.

"While the bridegroom tarried, they all slumbered and slept.

"And at midnight there was a cry made, Behold, the bridegroom cometh; go ye out to meet him.

"Then all those virgins arose, and trimmed their lamps.

"And the foolish said unto the wise, Give us of your oil; for our lamps are gone out.

"But the wise answered, saying, not so; lest there be not enough for us and you; but go ye rather to them that sell, and buy for yourselves.

"And while they went to buy, the bridegroom came; and they that were ready went in with him to the marriage: and the door was shut.

"Afterward came also the other virgins, saying, Lord, Lord, open to us.

"But he answered and said, Verily I say unto you, I know ye not.

"Watch therefore, for ye know neither the day nor the hour wherein the son of man cometh" (Matthew 25:1–13).

As a youth I wondered why the virgins who had ample portions of oil were unwilling to share with the unprepared ones. As I've grown older, I have come to understand that the oil could not be shared because in this case it was not a commodity.

Rather, this kind of oil lights the way to Jesus Christ and is accumulated over a lifetime of preparation through faith in and obedience to the principles of the gospel. How can one share their conversion?

The General Handbook of Instructions of The Church of Jesus Christ of Latter-day Saints, Section 22, advises us to follow prophetic counsel by putting our faith in Jesus Christ into action by "eliminating unnecessary debt, living within our means, and establishing family home storage and financial reserves."

Our faith further leads us to educate our minds and our hands and to strive daily to be self-reliant. Having taken care of our own needs, we are better able to provide for ourselves and serve others.

Obedience to the Lord's counsel brings temporal and spiritual blessings. It allows us to face the challenges of life armed with courage and confidence rather than fear and doubt (*General Handbook of Instructions*, Section 22, ChurchofJesusChrist.org).

I am grateful for such counsel, both the practical, daily kind and the serious, more weighty type. Following is a list of suggested actions, including practical, social, and spiritual matters, for your consideration:

Home Reserves

I try to maintain at least a three-month supply of the following items in my home:

- Food
- Water
- Fuel

It's wise to make a list of the items you would need to survive in an emergency such as medications and store at least a three-month supply in a secure place.

Another helpful act is to make a list of things you would want to take with you should you need to evacuate your home on short notice and that are not in your 72-hour kit.

This could include such items as eyeglasses, smart phone and charging cord, medications, hard drives with information on them, digitized photos, or a laptop computer.

Medical Care

It's advisable to keep medical information in a file for convenience and for the benefit of family members and caregivers. It could include the following:

- Contact information for doctors, technicians, nurses, and home health aids
- Addresses of near-by facilities
- Copies of advanced health and care directives (Forms are available online.)

Household and Property Maintenance

Because home and yard maintenance has become too physically demanding for me, I now:

- Engage a yard service for lawn mowing, edging, pruning, and leaf blowing.
- Have window washers come as needed.

- Have a house cleaning team come once a month to dust, vacuum, and clean bathroom and kitchen floors.
- Keep a list of "to do" items that family members can help with when they drop by.

Financial Affairs

My husband left our financial affairs in order, and the executor of the estate has access to important information, including login IDs and passwords. The information includes the following:

- Income
- Tithing
- Debts and obligations
- Savings
- Investments
- Taxes
- Automatic withdrawals
- Up-to-date wills and trust funds
- Legal transactions and counsel
- Comprehensive care, should the need arise

Disposition of Valuables

It can be helpful to decide in advance how you want to handle the disposition of valuable items. Personally, I want items gifted to me by a family member returned to the giver. For the rest, my attorney sons recommend the following:

"Dividing personal property among heirs can often lead to hurt feelings or even family feuds. One way to avoid this is to have a family auction, either with real money or 'house credit.' (House credit can be an amount that approximates what an heir's share of the estates' other assets would be.) The house-credit option obviously only works if the auction participants are limited to heirs.

"This might sound like a cold and overly business-like way to distribute personal property, but it is the best way we have heard to avoid potential disputes. With an auction, every heir has an equal opportunity to claim the items they want with the item going to the highest bidder. No one can complain if they do not get what they want, as they had the chance to bid higher.

"All the money raised in the auction goes back into the estate to be divided among the heirs. An experienced trusts and estates attorney can help you with the details."

Funeral Burial Preferences and Plans

Not only is the passing of a loved one difficult emotionally; it can also be a stress-filled time, and arrangements need to be made quickly. Some of the stress can be eliminated by good planning and preparation ahead of time. Consider the following:

- Purchase burial plots well in advance.

- Identify a preferred mortuary.

- Prepare a draft of the obituary.

- Have clothing prepared for burial.

- Plan the funeral program, naming the people for prayers and talks, specifying the hymns to be sung and special musical numbers.

- Decide who will dedicate the grave.

- Decide whether there will be a family lunch following the burial, and, if so, how it is to be prepared, served, set up, and cleaned up.

Social Situations for Widows and Widowers

It can be helpful for you who are widowed to seriously consider your social status at some point and determine the position you want to take as a "single" person.

Are you interested in dating and/or developing a romantic relationship or even entertaining the possibility of marriage? Or, like me, are you only interested in casual friendships with those of the opposite sex?

To avoid getting into a situation where I could be uncomfortable or cause misleading expectations for anyone, I have chosen to always wear my wedding ring.

Spiritual Readiness

I believe one of the most important things to consider is spiritual readiness. Spiritual preparedness can increase resilience and the ability to face life's challenges. It provides the peace and assurance that everything is in order.

In short, having a current temple recommend, which to me is a personal checklist of my standing before the Lord, and having a prophet to follow are extremely comforting to me in today's otherwise world of conflicts and challenges.

On a more specific basis, I, like millions of other members of The Church of Jesus Christ of Latter-day Saints, find comfort and strength in walking the covenant path. This leads me to keeping the commandments and honoring my covenants. It makes the sabbath a delight, highlighted by partaking of the sacrament each Sunday. I love the *"Come, Follow Me"* course of study and since my circumstances give me lots of discretionary time, I am able to augment the program with a personal study plan that includes additional scriptures, gospel books and podcasts, and the availability online of inspirational messages, such as general conference talks and other edifying messages that help prepare me for living in these times.

For example, a general conference address, *In Preparation for the Second Coming of the Savior*, by (then) Elder Dallin H. Oaks in April 2004 offers vital spiritual counsel as follows:

> "We are surrounded by challenges on all sides (see 2 Cor. 4:8–9). But with faith in God, we trust the blessings He has promised those who keep His commandments. We have faith in the future, and we are preparing for that future. To borrow a metaphor from the familiar world of athletic competitions, we do not know when this game will end, and we do

not know the final score, but we do know that when the game finally ends, our team wins. We will continue to go forward 'till the purposes of God shall be accomplished, and the Great Jehovah shall say the work is done" (History of the Church, 4:540).

"Wherefore," the Savior tells us, "Be faithful, praying always, having your lamps trimmed and burning, and oil with you, that you may be ready at the coming of the Bridegroom—For behold, verily, verily, I say unto you, that I come quickly" (Doctrine and Covenants 33:17–18).

There is no substitute for preparation.

I want to always be among those whose lamp is trimmed, for both temporal and spiritual purposes.

(Note: Please see Chapter 9, "Opting for Assisted Living" for detailed information on living in a care facility.)

CHAPTER SIX

Keeping Safety Rules

It's patch, patch, patch, or so it seems to me in trying to take care of myself as I grow older. It is also a matter of prevent and protect in this aging process. During my late eighties, my health began taking center stage and I became increasingly preoccupied with safety and wellness. Neither condition can be guaranteed; I can only take care of myself wisely, seek professional medical help as needed, and then do my best and trust that the rest will work out.

The following pages are about doing my best.

One summer day, I was rearranging a chair outside on the patio when suddenly I found myself face down on the brick surface. I was so stunned that I didn't move for a few seconds, but when I did turn over and sit up, I discovered I was in serious trouble. For the life of me I could not stand up. I struggled and struggled and tried every trick I knew, but I could not get on my feet.

In desperation, I pressed the rescue alert button hanging around my neck. A moment later a friendly voice was asking through my device if I was all right? Should she call 911 or just contact my emergency list of neighbors and family?

Fortunately, the latter would suffice. Within minutes, a kind neighbor entered my yard, prepared to comfort me until others arrived. The phone rang. It was my son Roger responding by saying, "I'm on the way!" Help was coming.

I have worn a rescue alert device day and night since Hank passed away in 2013 and I began living alone. For me, it is indispensable for my protection and peace of mind, and my neighbors and family members get benefits, too. Their awareness as to my circumstances around the clock provides peace of mind for them as well. Owning this medical device is like purchasing an insurance policy. If I need it or do not need it, I am a winner either way.

In addition to wearing the rescue alert button, there are other aids that contribute to our safety, convenience and comfort such as handrails, grab bars, walk-in showers, hand-held shower heads, stools or benches for the shower, toilet risers, grabbers for picking up items from high or low places, and ramps in place of stairs.

Walkers, canes, or walking sticks help prevent falling and increase strength and mobility. They also help you walk normally, rather than shuffle. I have found that the use of my walker has significantly enhanced the quality of my life, enabling me to go farther, faster, and safer than otherwise.

Exercise equipment can build strength and improve balance. Physical therapists can coach you in their use, either at home, through online podcasts, or at a local gymnasium for the greatest productivity.

Wheelchairs and bedside equipment may be necessary if you become incapacitated. Their use decreases your strength and limits your independence, but sometimes they are the only option outside of total bed confinement.

Photo of me in 2021 with my walker as I enjoy the beach with my daughter, Rebecca, at North Carolina's Outer Banks.

I grew up learning about the "survival of the fittest," and

while that is a truism in many situations, I think another "law" also has merit for us as we age, and that is the "survival of the one who adapts." I find myself making adaptations from minor to major on an almost daily basis.

This matter of adapting, as it turns out, can be fun as I become a little creative in solving problems. Here is one about a case in point:

I have a basement laundry room with a steep stairway leading to it. Instead of carrying a full basket of laundry down the steps which causes me to feel unbalanced as I do so, I have exchanged my laundry basket for a laundry bag that can be tossed down the stairs and safely picked up at the bottom and dragged to the washer.

Below is another story that addresses the need for doing things differently from what I would otherwise prefer:

The Half-On Lids

There was my granddaughter Abby, full of good intentions, systematically going through my cupboards and straightening and tightening jar lids on bottles along each shelf. I was afraid she thought "Grandma has really lost it. What happened to neatness and order in her house?"

I caught her before she completed the task, and we both laughed as I explained that the lids were crooked and loose intentionally because that was the only way I could open them with my arthritic hands. Abby promptly retraced her steps, loosening lids as she went.

I try to protect myself from awkward situations or harm and danger in every possible way by making lifestyle adaptations and adjustments. Here is another example from an incident before I started using a walker:

Look Up, Sister, Look Up

"Look up, sister, look up," called a woman to me as I passed her in the hall of the temple on my way to the dressing room to prepare for my shift in the sealing office. Her well-intended, but misplaced remark gave me pause for reflection.

I wanted to reply, "I know I am looking down at the floor with my head bent as I walk along, but I am looking up with my heart as I anticipate the sweet, sacred service opportunity ahead of me.

I'm looking down at the floor due to the fact that in my old age I've developed a fear of falling, and not without reason because I have experienced several bad tumbles. I try not to obsess about it, but I have learned to be cautious wherever I walk. I stumble easily, and I often feel a little wobbly and off balance. Sometimes I drag my feet, rather than lift them up. I, therefore, watch where I am going and how I am doing it. I know it's better to look up, but in unfamiliar territory it may be the wisest to look down.

Life for me as an almost 90-year-old widow with some physical limitations requires lots of adaptations and adjustments. In many ways, it's a "one day at a time," "figure it out as you go along," "measure your step," kind of season for me.

Accidents happen despite our best efforts. It makes sense, however, to minimize the chances of misfortune as much as possible by being careful, remaining on the alert, keeping safety rules, and making lifestyle adaptations and adjustment as advisable.

Compliance with this home safety checklist is caution in action:

- Wear sensible shoes, ones that are sturdy and supportive.
- Wear a rescue alert device.
- Create a safe, secure environment.
- Maintain order inside and outside.

- Install motion-sensitive outdoor lights along the driveway and as needed in the yard.

- Keep repairs up to date.

- Make sure walkways and doorways are free from obstructions.

- Use sturdy furniture.

- Check appliances for correct use.

- Secure or remove carpets and rugs to avoid tripping.

- Keep electrical cords out of the way.

- Install handrails along stairways.

- Install grab bars in the bathroom.

- Use a hand-held shower head.

- Avoid sharp edges.

- Be wary of slippery floors.

Following is a list of adjustments for your consideration:

- Have groceries, medications, etc. delivered.

- Select less-busy driving times and safer routes.

- Avoid nighttime driving, if possible.

- Simplify food preparation.

- Convert household lighting to LED lighting and leave some lights on all night for safety.

- Leave lights on when going out in order to avoid coming home to a dark house.

- Choose clothing and shoes that are easy to put on and take off.

- Use the seat on your walker as more than a rest stop. It can be handy for transporting laundry, trash, groceries, books, dinner trays, and similar items about the house and yard.

The above is a "word of warning to the wise" as you "patch" and "prevent" and "protect" as necessary. I hope for blessings to you in your efforts to be safe.

In summation, I gratefully accept these prophetic words to live by: "Your physical body is a magnificent creation of God. It is his temple as well as yours and must be treated with reverence" (Russell M. Nelson, "Self-Mastery," *General Conference,* October 1985).

CHAPTER SEVEN

Striving For Physical and Mental Health

*T*he circus is coming to town!" I was ecstatic. It was 1939 and the "greatest show on earth," namely the Ringling Brothers and Barnum & Bailey Circus, would perform in my very city.

I was beside my five-year-old self with anticipation and excitement as I pictured in my mind the Big Top (tent) with its three gigantic rings or centers for circus entertainment. There would be the elephant parade on Main Street with the animals and their trainers, the funny clowns in their polka dot suits and big red noses mingling with the crowd, and the daring trapeze artists who defy the law of gravity as the spectators hold their collective breath and while the performers do back flips high in the air. I counted the days, more like the hours, until such a thrill of a lifetime would be mine.

Then one day everything suddenly came to a crushing halt. It was over before it even started. My father announced that he had returned the tickets and that our family would not be attending the circus.

Polio had broken out in the area and people would not be gathering in large groups where germs could spread. I was devastated.

Children everywhere were inconsolably disappointed. Some had a hard time understanding what the crippling effects of polio had to do with the fun of a circus. A little girl in our neighborhood tried to convince her parents that it would be okay for her to go to the circus if she took crutches.

Horror stories circulated widely about people dying or being crippled for life or, worst of all, being confined to an iron lung for the rest of their lives.

There was a man up the street from our home in an iron lung from the last round of polio. We could see him through the window of his house with his head poking out of a life-size metal tube that somehow breathed for him. Thoughts of him and his huge respirator haunted me.

Well, that was more than 80 years ago. Polio is no longer a deadly threat. I recall clearly the global relief and mass gratitude that prevailed when, in 1955, successful results were announced from a vaccine created by US physician, Jonas Salk.

In addition to this miraculous advance in medical science, measles and similar debilitating diseases continued to be virtually eradicated through immunization.

Other illnesses could be treated and cured. Hearts and lungs could be transplanted. I, myself, walk without pain on two titanium knees.

Due to highly specialized and rapidly advancing methods and a vast amount of information available in medicine, many people are healthier and living longer than ever before. It is definitely to our advantage that we be informed and take as much advantage as possible of each step leading us to better treatments, even cures.

We all know it is beneficial to practice a healthy lifestyle by eating properly, sleeping adequately, exercising regularly, and controlling our weight. We understand the importance of being proactive and staying current with immunization such as getting an annual flu shot and following medical counsel regarding all vaccinations.

It is important to take the initiative and arrange an annual wellness check-up with your primary care physician. This examination should extend to laboratory procedures and any scopes and scans advisable.

It could be lifesaving to see a dermatologist for potentially dangerous skin spots.

It is wise to undergo yearly vision and hearing evaluations.

We smile with understanding as we age that a frequent "complaint" among our peers is we often have too much room in the house, but not enough space in the medicine cabinet.

Seriously, however, not only is taking care of our physical health important as we grow older, mental illnesses such as depression and anxiety are on the rise afflicting one in six people. Understanding mental health and mental illness is of great significance to seniors.

Even though these illnesses are more common in today's world, it does not mean they are a normal part of aging. Quite often when symptoms of depression and anxiety are exhibited by a senior, their loved ones, believing this is typical, ignore the signs. This is unfortunate because there is help for everyone.

I have a close-up understanding of mental illness because my daughter, Elaine, was diagnosed at the age of 29 with what is now termed Major Depressive Disorder (MDD) and General Anxiety Disorder (GAD). Through Elaine's 30- year journey with debilitating depression, accompanying anxiety, countless treatments, and extensive experience with doctors and therapists, she has become a passionate advocate for people suffering from similar conditions.

Elaine is now a certified peer support specialist and is a speaker for The National Alliance on Mental Illness (NAMI.) She offers hope, help, and healing through her informative website elainehquinn.com and her insightful, recently published book, *It's Time—Living a Full and Joyful Life With Depression and Anxiety.*

Elaine writes, "Depression and anxiety are real illnesses that are painful, disabling, and life threatening. Thinking of them in any other way is a far-reaching mistake. These illnesses are diagnosable and treatable. No one should have to suffer from them unnecessarily. The good news is that more and more

research is being done in the mental health field. There is already a lot of help available.

"The key in treating depression and anxiety is to recognize it early in yourself or someone else. The symptoms of these illnesses, according to the Anxiety and Depression Association of America (ADAA) include the following evidence:

- Persistent sad, anxious, or "empty" mood
- Feelings of hopelessness or pessimism
- Feelings of guilt, worthlessness, or helplessness
- Loss of interest or pleasure in hobbies and activities, including sex
- Decreased energy, fatigue, or feeling "slowed down"
- Difficulty concentrating, remembering, or making decisions
- Insomnia or early morning awakening
- Low appetite and weight loss or overeating and weight gain
- Thoughts of death or suicide or suicide attempts
- Restlessness or irritability
- Persistent physical symptoms that do not respond to treatment, such as headaches, digestive disorders, and pain for which no other cause can be diagnosed

"If you have experienced two or more of these symptoms for two weeks, it is wise to contact your primary care doctor for a diagnosis and treatment. Evidence-based research confirms that a combination of medication and cognitive therapy is what is needed to resolve mental illness."

Elaine further advises, "Medication has been an important first step for me and is like a springboard allowing me to take further steps to find healing and wellness."

Following are six remedies Elaine adapted to the elderly for the purpose of my book on aging:

1. **Sleep well.** Depression throws off our body rhythms which disturb sleep patterns. Getting a full eight to nine hours of restful sleep each night helps to put your body rhythms in sync and heal from depression. Your doctor will have some ideas for you to accomplish this.

2. **Eat healthily.** Another body rhythm is feeling hungry. Depression can cause overeating or a lack of appetite. Eating a balanced diet is important to good mental health. Again, work with your doctor to discover ways to eat well.

3. **Move your body.** It is well stated that "Motion is like lotion for the brain." Even a short, slow walk can do wonders for your mental health. Don't use old age as an excuse to sit and do nothing. Do something daily to move your body. Movement can also include moving your arms and legs from a sitting position. Go to YouTube and search tutorials you can follow for different ways to move your body. (Ask someone for help with technology if you don't know how to access YouTube.)

4. **Cultivate a sense of belonging.** Most everyone's mental health is boosted when they feel loved and know they belong. Elderly people can feel especially lonely if they live alone and have lost close family members and friends. It requires courage to reach out to others for this kind of support. Yet if you do you will find it worth the effort to do such things as attend church, go to community activities, be present at extended family events, and visit with neighbors. You can Zoom and FaceTime with loved ones around the country.

5. **Enjoy a hobby.** Depression also takes away enjoyment. Make an effort to do the things you have liked in the past, even if you feel unmotivated to do them

at first. You may fulfill a church calling you enjoy. You can engage in family history and temple work. You can spend time with grandchildren. Maybe you would like to take care of a pet. You can also develop a new hobby. In fact, there was a woman who learned to understand and hence appreciate opera while being confined to her bed.

6. **Have a sense of purpose.** Having a connection with a sense of purpose in your life brings about mental health and wellness. As members of the Church our relationship with our Heavenly Father and the Savior can give us this sense of purpose. You can spend time in prayer and meditation. You can write in your journal and work on your life story. You can ponder over the scriptures. You can serve others in simple ways. With today's technology there are endless podcasts and talks you can listen to for a spiritual boost. These types of activities are wonderful contributors to good mental health.

Elaine concludes by stating: "I have seen for myself that even my simple efforts to help bring about good mental health have made a huge difference for good. I agree with the thought from Alma 37:6, '*Behold I say unto you, that by small and simple things are great things brought to pass.*' I just keep trying and never give up and this has made it so I live a life full of joy. Winston Churchill said it this way: 'Continuous effort, not strength or intelligence, is the key to unblocking our potential.' I know this statement to be true."

It is vitally important in today's complex, stress-filled, and rapidly changing world that you and I are our own physical and mental health advocate: informed, up to date, involved, and responsible.

With regards to our physical and mental health, it is important to strive to live life fully and not let our health, physically or mentally, define us. It is best to avoid the organ recital. No, not the kind where we listen to fine music. Rather it is the type where "oldies" sit around and repeatedly recite the details of their diseases and surgeries and rehearse the aches and pains of their internal organs.

Above all, I am deeply grateful that we, as members of The Church of Jesus Christ of Latter-day Saints, can rely on scientific methods *and* the power of prayer and priesthood administrations in facing physical and mental health problems. We can expect miracles through faith in the Lord, Jesus Christ, the Great Physician and Healer. In every circumstance, we are taught to pray always (Doctrine and Covenants 90:24) and that all things should be done in wisdom and order (Mosiah 4:27).

We are greatly blessed to live during such a time as this when medical science can work wonders in our lives. Even though there is much more that needs to be done, the future is growing brighter for everyone.

"And all saints who remember to keep and do these sayings, walking in obedience to the commandments, shall receive health in their navel and marrow to their bones; and shall find wisdom and great treasures of knowledge, even hidden treasures; and shall run and not be weary and shall walk and not faint. And I, the Lord, give unto them a promise, that the destroying angel shall by pass them, as the children of Israel, and not slay them. Amen."

Doctrine and Covenants 89:18–21

CHAPTER EIGHT

Lessening Loneliness In Your Life

Holidays are all about spending time with loved ones, and I look forward to each occasion with high anticipation. Usually, the Fourth of July means cheering family members on in a 5K race or a marathon and then gathering for a barbecue and watching fireworks. One year, however, was different for me, when everyone in my large, attentive family was away or busy with their own activities. I found myself with no plans for the long holiday weekend. It is easy at such times to feel empty and sad with some anxiety and experience a little fear of abandonment. It is lonely.

It's safe to assume that everybody has experienced loneliness at some time and to some degree in our lives. We can feel it even when we are surrounded by people if there is an absence of a connection between us. One can feel lonely in a crowded room. As Brené Brown said, "In the absence of love and connection there is always suffering."

Loneliness is a challenging problem that can affect our physical and mental health. An article in *Everyday Health* explains that "loneliness, by definition, is the state of distress or discomfort that results when one perceives a gap between one's desires for social connection and the actual experience of it." (everydayhealth.com/loneliness)

If you are struggling with loneliness, proactively addressing the problem can help alleviate it. For example, a widowed friend was feeling sorry for herself as she sat alone at church, when it occurred to her that she could end the "pity party" by getting up and sitting by someone. It was such a simple action, but it changed her whole outlook on the situation.

If you desire connection, you can be the one to reach out to someone else. It may take courage and you may feel vulnerable, but there is little to lose and much to gain. As clinical psychologist

Sue Johnson said, "That is the ultimate human dilemma. Risk and you could be hurt, rejected, and abandoned. Don't risk and you could be alone forever."

> That is the ultimate human dilemma. Risk and you could be hurt, rejected, and abandoned. Don't risk and you could be alone forever.
>
> --Sue Johnson

It is important to keep in mind that feelings of loneliness are normal. According to Stephanie Cacioppo, PhD, assistant professor of psychiatry and behavioral neuroscience at the University of Chicago, "Feeling lonely isn't necessarily a bad thing. It's a reminder that something's off about your social environment and that you need to prioritize your happiness." However, if the feelings become excessive, overwhelming, or interfere with daily life, professional help should be sought.

There are ways to address loneliness and to help develop meaningful connections in our lives, even in our older years. Some of the things discussed in other chapters can help alleviate feelings of loneliness, such as recording daily impressions of the Lord's hand in your life. Here are some proactive steps to take:

- Keep a gratitude journal. Focusing on the good in your life will have positive consequences, including having a cheerful countenance.

- Along the same lines, make a habit of giving people you pass throughout the day a cheerful smile. This simple act can have profound benefits for you and the other person, helping you both feel connected and creating a bond between you, if only for a moment.

- Take a class. Many community colleges, libraries, museums, or even craft stores offer classes. This is a good opportunity not only to learn something new, but to meet people from different walks of life. Your life will be enriched.

- Volunteer with a local service organization. Again, this is a likely chance to meet people from different walks of life. Consider mentoring a college student from a disadvantaged background. Multi-generational friendships can be very rewarding.

- Identify someone from your neighborhood that you would like to know better, then invite them to

> Sometimes your joy is the source of your smile, but sometimes your smile can be the source of your joy."
>
> -Tich Nhat Hanh

join you for a walk or other activity. It's possible that person is feeling lonely, too, and will appreciate your reaching out.

- Arrange a group to get together monthly for lunch at a local restaurant.

- Attend church and church activities. Do your ministering with the intent of truly getting to know and love the person you are assigned to.

- Connect with family members near and far on a regular basis through phone calls, FaceTime, or other technology.

- Reframe your attitude. Think of your loneliness as solitude, which is a choice. Solitude at certain times and in certain places can be enjoyable, even therapeutic. Think of your alone times as a chance to reconnect with yourself, with nature, or to tackle a project.

I am grateful to know that even on the days when we feel the loneliest, we are never truly alone. I know that Heavenly Father is aware of me and is in the details of my life. I can look to him for comfort and inspiration. I can receive the help and strength that I need to reach out to others with love and to create relationships that will bless and enrich my life.

CHAPTER NINE

Opting For Assisted Living

"So, how old do you have to be before you can move in?" laughed Jennifer, my niece, as she was inquiring at an assisted care facility on behalf of her aging parents. She was feeling "blown away" by the attractive, immaculately clean building; the graciousness and efficiency of the staff; the long list of service offerings; and the many amenities available. She felt a bit envious of the senior citizens living there in such comfort, convenience, and security. It would be ideal for her mom and dad, under their circumstances.

Granted, there is no place like home. But when "home" is no longer adequate, what is next? Engaging a home nursing service? Moving in with family? Down-sizing to a small, one-level house? Moving nearer to family members? Relocating to some type of long-term care facility?

This can be an extremely dreaded and difficult decision, one that I and many other "oldies" must eventually face. It is a personal, individual matter, not a case of "one size fits all."

A friend who chose to remarry and move with her new husband to a homeowner's association (HOA) neighborhood remarked: "I cannot tell you how energizing it is to meet and love new people and be relieved of the burden of yard work, snow removal, and home repairs."

My sister Donette and brother-in-law Gail Ockey, in their eighties and facing increasing health challenges, reached the point where living at home on their own was no longer "doable." After family discussions and a thorough consideration of circumstances and options, they, with the support of their children, decided that the best choice for them was to relocate to a long-term assisted care facility.

It was a bonus feature, they felt, that they could make the decision as a couple and then act upon it together. In this way they, at the new location, could make new friends, establish new traditions, and create new memories. Most importantly, if one required hospitalization or rehabilitative care due to a fall or a stroke or other emergency, there is help already in place for the other.

This major decision leads to many more big issues to consider, such as financing and location. Other things to consider are the extent of services required: assisted care, full care, or memory care? What about the proximity to family members? Inquire about the number of rooms and their size. Ask about the amenities in private and public areas, furnishings, parking space if needed, medical care and equipment, and how medications are handled.

Meal service is of prime importance. In other words, "What's for dinner?" can be a deal maker or breaker in the decision process. Is food served at the table or is it cafeteria style? Is it permissible to invite guests to join you in the dining room for a meal at a small cost?

What can you expect from a cleaning team that maintains the individual apartments?

What about laundry facilities? Many places provide magnetic room numbers to put on the washer and dryer so a resident can remember which machines their clothes occupy.

There are other considerations which are of lesser importance but still of significance inasmuch as this facility will become the resident's "world," and it should be to their liking as much as possible.

For instance, would you be interested in "a room with a view?" If so, what do you prefer seeing through your windows?

When my siblings and I were helping my widowed father, Don Van Dam, settle in an assisted care facility in the Millcreek area of Salt Lake City, we initially thought he would prefer a second-floor apartment looking toward the magnificent Wasatch Mountain Range where the great Mt. Olympus was artfully "framed" by the sitting room window. The change of seasons, as enjoyed by looking at the mountains, would add color and beauty; it was scenic nature at its best.

Not so, however, for Dad. He signed up for a main floor apartment that featured the parking lot. He loved to see cars come and go and people enter and leave the building. The motion—the action of life being lived—appealed to him.

My brother-in-law Rudy and sister-in-law Alice Hoole have a room with a view from their assisted care facility in Payson, Utah. It boasts a splendid shot of the beautiful temple, less than a mile away. They love to join other residents of the facility once each month for a temple excursion.

What about church services? Some facilities hold a brief non-denominational worship service each week. Others in the Intermountain West have independent branches of The Church of Jesus Christ of Latter-day Saints which provide sacrament meeting, Sunday School, and priesthood meeting and Relief Society.

In his nineties, my father attended the meetings faithfully each Sunday at the care center and enjoyed participating. He especially liked passing the sacrament and recalled how he did that as a young boy in the Wandamere Ward of Salt Lake City. As he talked to me, he would smile and add that the story of his extensive service in the Church during his lifetime could be titled, "From Deacon to Deacon."

Almost every facility has a common room, game tables (often with a pool table), an arts and craft center, a puzzle center, a gym, and a library area.

Only a short walk down the hall, there is usually a doctor, a dentist, a podiatrist, a nurse, physical or occupational therapy instructors, a salon with a hairstylist/barber, and an on-site handyman. A driver with a van is available for

Finding A Home

Medicare.gov makes it easy to find and compare nursing homes in your area and what they do and do not cover. Personalize your results by filtering for what matters most to you - inspection results, location, quality ratings, etc.

When comparing nursing homes:

* Check out their overall star ratings based on three areas: health inspections, staffing, and quality of resident care.

* View detailed staffing data including staffing levels and turnover rates.

* Find nursing home contact information and directions by visiting medicare.gov.

transportation for errands, appointments, sight-seeing—outings of various types.

There are movies, guest speakers, performers, book reviews, book exchange programs, and art and craft classes. Workshops for wood carving, photography, or writing may be conducted.

There is frequently someone at the piano or strumming a guitar in the lobby. Residents gather around the fireplace to chat. A garden stroll or watching the sunset from a bench in the yard are popular pastimes.

Snacks, such as ice cream cones and bags of freshly buttered popcorn, are regularly available in the common area. Visiting grandchildren love the treats.

Often there is a friend nearby or someone wanting a friend. There is always the quiet and privacy of your own room—your own space, with a book, TV, or computer—and a nap.

Residents are encouraged to arrange their apartment like "home" with their own furnishings, wall hangings, knick-knacks—their favorite things. Shelves can be added, if desired. They are free in many facilities to decorate their doors and a small area outside the door to give personality and individuality to their space.

No matter how satisfactory living conditions may be—home nursing service, increased help from your family or others, or residence in a care facility—there are always challenges to be faced and adjustments to be made. That is part of life, wherever you live, and regardless of your age. Look for the best and you will find it. Make it your "home sweet home."

Gift Idea

Adult children whose parents reside in an assisted care facility may find the following gift idea shared by Sharilyn Green useful in their own situation:

My Christmas gift to my parents this year was to purchase in advance the dinner coupons available for visitors at their assisted living center. I selected a cute little box and filled it with pre-purchased coupons so that when visitors come to eat with them, a pre-paid meal coupon is ready to go. I can restock the box for all gift-giving holidays to come. It's hard to think of good gifts at this stage in their life so I was super happy (and so were they) with my idea.

CHAPTER TEN

Seeking Life Long Learning

My husband, Hank, experienced a learning incident as a teenager that transformed his life. It happened in his birth city, Amsterdam. The year was 1946, and the Dutch were still picking up pieces from World War II which had crumbled to a close for them the year before. He had recently been baptized a member of The Church of Jesus Christ of Latter-day Saints, the only one of his family to do so at the time. He was what you could call a "walk-in" convert.

This is his story as he related it to me:

For want of something to do one evening he and three other youths from his neighborhood had wandered into a building where his companions told him anyone was welcome to enter and play table tennis on Tuesday evenings. The people he met were so nice and he had such a good time that he went back the next week, and the next week, and the next week until he became "one with them."

This building happened to be the location of a branch of The Church of Jesus Christ of Latter-day Saints. What transpired for Hank the next few months is legendary, but that is a story for another time. I want to tell you a story within the story for the purposes of this chapter.

One evening at MIA (Mutual), as he stood with the group to recite the theme, the scripture was Doctrine and Covenants 93:36.

"The glory of God is intelligence, or, in other words, light and truth."

Doctrine and Covenants 93: 36-37

He was struck with such a force as he heard it that it changed him forever. He experienced a total paradigm shift in his thinking, living, and goal setting.

Hank had dropped out of school in the fourth grade, after repeating the class twice, due to his lack of interest and the chaotic war conditions that surrounded him. He had planned on joining the Dutch navy when he became of age and going to sea.

But now he suddenly felt entirely different; plans for his future changed on the spot. A desire for an education flooded over him.

It was a few years, however, before he could put attaining a formal education into practice. He first emigrated to the United States three years later and settled with other Dutch immigrants in Salt Lake City. Next, he answered a draft call and served in the US army for two years during the Korean War. Then he returned to his homeland to fulfill a two-year mission for the Church.

Upon his return, he entered the University of Utah at age 25 as a freshman. With no formal education in between, it was a big leap from the fourth grade in Dutch to the university in English, but he succeeded and was graduated with a Bachelor of Science degree in business four years later. He commenced what turned out to be a highly successful career in life insurance and estate planning.

Meanwhile, we were married and began our family.

Photo shows Hank and me on his graduation day in 1959 with our toddler, Jean, and our baby, Roger.

Education, both informal and formal, both secular and spiritual, is of course strongly encouraged—actually highly emphasized—by The Church of Jesus Christ of Latter-day Saints. Education, as it is defined, is an intentional, purposeful act for the acquisition of knowledge, skills, and character traits. It is the training of our minds and hands for various purposes. It is about developing the powers of reason and judgment and generally preparing ourselves for mature life.

Ongoing learning can be a way of life. It is never too late to learn more. We live in a wonderful time when opportunities for learning surround us. Elder Robert D. Hales had this to say:

> "A few of the basic attributes to become a lifelong learner are courage, faithful desire, humility, patience, curiosity, and a willingness to communicate and share knowledge that we gain. . . . Lifelong learning is essential to the vitality of the human

mind, body, and soul. It enhances self-worth and self-actuation" ("The Journey of Lifelong Learning," *Brigham Young University Speeches,* 2009).

I find that looking back to our great leaders of the past encourages me to engage in some forward thinking. The following words from Joseph F. Smith, for example, offer food for thought:

"The mere stuffing of the mind with a knowledge of facts is not education. The mind must not only possess a knowledge of the truth, but the soul must reveal it, cherish it, love it as a priceless gem; and this human life must be guided and shaped by it in order to fulfill its destiny" (Joseph F. Smith, *Gospel Doctrine: Selections from the Sermons and Writings of Joseph F. Smith,* p. 269)

My niece, Sharilyn Green, is one who has gone back to school to finish her degree at age 60, and she has hardly left her home computer to do so. Actually, it was by looking up Grandma Moses on *Wikipedia* and reading about all that she accomplished later in life that Sharilyn found the encouragement and motivation to sign up for classes. In short, this is the gist of what she read:

Grandma Moses was an American folk painter. She was no stranger to hardship and loss. Five of her ten children died in infancy, and she was widowed at the age of 67.

Grandma Moses loved to embroider but because of painful arthritis switched to painting instead. When her right hand began to hurt, she changed to her left hand.

At the age of 78 she began painting in earnest, eventually creating over 1500 works of art.

In her autobiography (which she published at the age of 92), she said, "I look to my life like a good day's work, it was fine, and I feel satisfied with it. I was happy and content. I knew nothing better and made the best of what life offered. And life is what we make of it, always has been, always will."

Grandma Moses died in 1961 at the age of 101.

The story of Grandma Moses is inspiring. We don't need to begin a new career at the age of 78, but we can continue to grow and progress.

We can take advantage of community and church-sponsored classes, study groups, libraries, and other resources.

I enjoy learning at home by reading good books, and by attending classes, listening to or watching a wide range of documentaries, podcasts, and lecture series online. I appreciate other virtual or in-person learning experiences in the arts, cultures, travels, biographies, histories, editorials, and especially about the gospel of Jesus Christ in the scriptures.

I like associating with people who share their knowledge, and I like learning from life itself as I watch the world turn, so to speak, all around me.

Following is a list of suggested good study habits for Seniors:

- Have a purpose in mind
- Avoid distractions
- Make notes
- Sit upright in a hard chair
- Place study material on a firm surface for support
- Wear reading glasses and/or hearing aids if necessary

- Use memory aids/mnemonics
- Discuss/share what you have learned with others
- Reread and repeat
- Take breaks

It is vitally important for our spiritual progression to make certain that the information is in harmony with the word of God as found in the scriptures and revealed doctrine as taught by our inspired leaders.

As I ponder the vast scope of learning opportunities available to us in the twenty-first century, I am grateful for the guidelines the Lord has provided for us as we make our selections. We recognize them as the last part of the 13th Article of Faith. It reads:

"If there is anything virtuous, lovely, or of good report, or praiseworthy, we seek after these things."

Learning has picked up a problem along the way for some of us, and that is re-membering what we have just heard or read. Sometimes I have to pause a few seconds and think hard to recall what was said a moment ago. I try to accept prompts graciously. Hopefully a little humor can be redeeming. I plan to recite the following verse the next time I need it. That's if I haven't forgotten it:

My bills are washed,
Laundry is paid,
Clothes are baking,
And dinner is in the dryer.
I got this!

CHAPTER ELEVEN

Enhancing Our Life Through Technology

A new recipe, a clever kitchen gadget, a handy household tool, a more efficient way of doing something, a breakthrough in medicine, or almost anything new and improved always interested me. I was usually quick to check it out and frequently made it "mine."

But it was different when the computer came along. The computer was of no interest to me. I had an electric typewriter that was more than adequate—or so I rationalized.

The thought "If it ain't broke, don't fix it" came to mind. My typewriter wasn't broken, and it didn't need fixing. My typewriter and I had been a productive duo for more than

Me and my beloved red typewriter

40 years. There was absolutely no reason, from my point of view, for intervention between me and my typewriter.

Hank, who fell easily for the computer, had a lot to say to me about its advantages and capabilities as he gallantly carried his new laptop back and forth between home and office. Never mind that at first he frequently had to seek "tech" support from our children—and worse, the grandchildren. Even the neighbors were on his call list. Not me. I could do it all, all by myself—on my trusty typewriter.

Speaking of children, mine were relentless in urging me to learn to use a computer. Actually, it was beyond that. They even suggested I get rid of my typewriter. One son, Spencer, offered to dispose of it for me.

Unthinkable.

Well, one day he came to visit and when he left, my typewriter was gone. It was nowhere to be seen. It had completely disappeared. I never saw it again.

It took me a long time to forgive him.

Now, I am grateful— really, really grateful that Spencer forced me into the world of technology. Along with indoor plumbing, technology is a gift to mankind.

I am thankful for a mother who was one to check out anything "new and possibly improved" that came along. She backed this willingness to venture into untried territory by telling us children that "One's age could be determined by the degree of pain they felt when coming in contact with a new idea."

In this way I want to be young and teachable.

Learning to use much of the technology that is available has greatly enhanced my life and enriched my relationship with others. I can instantly and easily connect with family and friends all over the world. Just keeping up with birthday greetings for my large family is fast and fun.

Family history work can be done online from the comfort of our homes. Photos, slides, and family records can be digitized.

YouTube tutorials can teach us how to do just about anything from fixing a leaking faucet to painting a scene in watercolor.

Streaming devices allow us to watch anything from entertaining movies to educational documentaries on demand.

Researched material and notes for lessons and talks and as well as for my own, personal edification are at my fingertips.

One of the silver linings of the COVID-19 Pandemic is that it forced us to use technology in ways that we might not have been comfortable with before. Early in the pandemic our family decided to get together one Sunday evening each month for a Zoom call. I had never heard of Zoom before and the first few times a grandson had to come over and show me how to connect the call. Now I am not only able to see and speak to family members who live nearby, I can also feel close to family members from across the country and "attend" special occasions such as baby blessings and baptisms.

In addition to Zoom calls, I have a monthly WhatsApp chat meeting with a sister-in-law, Marijke, in the Netherlands. It's almost as good as a visit in person.

I am glad I've lived long enough to see countless benefits from, what to me are miraculous, advances in communication and information. I have come a long way since the red typewriter episode. Not only is there a computer on my desk; I carry with me other electronic devices that I would be hard pressed to live without, such as a do-it-all phone around my neck and a very smart watch on my wrist.

Because of technology, I am able to help with the gathering of Israel on both sides of the veil.

It is true—it bears repeating--computers are a gift to humanity, including me. The sky is the limit.

CHAPTER TWELVE

Making It A Record Year: Write Your Life Story

My young great-granddaughter Alli was absorbed in her reading. In fact, she could hardly put the book down. While on the other side of the country, my eldest son, Roger, was reading a copy of the very same book to his youngest son, Tanner, at bedtime. The book they were reading was *Unfaltering Faith: The Life Story of Hendricus J.M. Hoole, Jr.* Not exactly a New York Times bestseller, my husband's life story still proved to be captivating reading for our grandchildren and great-grandchildren.

Whether you refer to such a record as a life story, a personal history, or something casual and simple such as "My Memories," recording highlights from your life is important to do. If you have already prepared something, congratulate yourself; if not, you may find the report printed below from Emory University compelling. Then the pages that follow in this chapter may provide some "how to" pointers.

"An Emory University study by psychologists Robyn Fivush and Marshall Duke indicated that knowing the stories of their ancestors helped children become more resilient. Similar studies also support the fact that there is a direct correlation between families that have a narrative and children who are not only resilient, but who feel secure, who have a sense of self-esteem and who are more inclined to thrive and are happy."

Following is a report, via *LDS Living*, on some of these findings:

> "The value of preserving and sharing ancestral stories was recently verified by researchers who were trying to understand why some people, including children, are better able than others to cope with serious, even disabling stress and trauma. One study found that 'the more children knew about their family's history, the stronger their sense of control over their lives, [and] the higher their self-esteem.' This factor was indeed 'the best single predictor of children's emotional health and happiness.' Those

with 'the most self-confidence' had what one researcher called a 'strong intergenerational self.' They know they belong to something bigger than themselves. A related study found that even among those affected by the tragedy of September 11, 2001, the people who 'knew more about their families proved to be more resilient, meaning they could moderate the effects of stress.' And the most helpful family stories are those that speak candidly and fairly about weathering life's natural 'ups and downs,' rather than exaggerating positive or negative attitudes or events in an unrealistic way. Thus, concludes writer Bruce Feiler, 'create, refine and retell the story of your family's positive moments and your ability to bounce back from the difficult ones. That act alone may increase the odds that your family will thrive for many generations to come.'"

(Hafen, Bruce C., and Marie K. Hafen. "Studies Show How Family History Makes Children More Resilient, Confident, and Happy." LDS Living, October 28, 2021)

Furthermore, we write to connect generations—to establish continuity over the years and to encourage preservation of historical information and pictures. We write to make memories, build character and provide learning. We write for enjoyment—theirs and ours.

A Life Story is a personal record of our experiences, attitudes, values, priorities, and—above all—our faith in the Lord, seeing His hand in our life, and our testimony of the gospel of Jesus Christ to pass on to our posterity. We write to build faith.

President Henry B. Eyring has made his habit of daily journal writing an opportunity to strengthen his testimony and the testimonies of his family. President Eyring said,

> "...Before I would write, I pondered this question: 'Have I seen the hand of God reaching out to touch us or our children or our family today?' As I kept at it, something began to happen. As I would cast my mind over the day, I would see evidence of what God had done for one of us that I had not recognized in the busy moments of the day. As that happened, and it happened often, I realized that trying to remember had allowed God to show me what He had done." (Henry B. Eyring, "O, Remember, Remember," *General Conference*, October 2007)

Our life stories can be our personal scriptures. As Nephi wrote on the small plates.

> "Upon these I write the things of my soul ... for the learning and profit of my children."

2 Nephi 4:15

I hope that by reading my life story, my posterity will come to understand the things of my soul and know that I have a testimony of my Savior, Jesus Christ and that I endeavored to be a valiant follower.

Taking liberty with Book of Mormon terminology, I have found the following three types of record keeping helpful for me as I have worked on my life story over the years:

"The Plate": A one- to two-page document consisting of a sketch or brief resume of one's life.

"The Small Plates": A record of approximately 100 pages with some facts, stories, examples, and a few photos from one's life. It can be contained in a folder or thin binder or digitized.

"The Large Plates": A more complete record, consisting of several hundred pages about one's life and family. It can be preserved in a box, loose-leaf binder, bound book, or digital format.

There is no "wrong way" to record and preserve your memoirs. Handwritten, typed, audio, video—whatever works best for you. As just explained, you can record only the essentials on a single page, or you can elaborate and fill a book. Either way, it will bless your posterity for generations.

There are some general guidelines for telling your story:

- Be honest; tell the truth, then everyone can learn and grow.

- Be kind; avoid being judgmental or critical.

- Seek permission if the information about others might be confidential or sensitive.

- Tell stories, give examples; facts and figures are important, but it is stories that are remembered and cherished.

At the time Hank was writing his life story, *Unfaltering Faith*, I also completed mine, *A Living Testimony: Stories from the Life of Daryl Van Dam Hoole*. We had a good time working on these projects together as we gathered photos and reminisced on the past. We ended up with beautiful, hard-bound books and presented them to our children and grandchildren on our 80th birthdays.

My personal application is a hybrid or combination between the life sketch and the story style. I wrote a two-page life sketch, or timeline, with facts and figures and a one-page testimony, which I considered to be "book ends" at the front and back of the book with 300 pages of stories and pictures in between.

It is never too early or too late to write your life story. To get started, it may be helpful to google some story prompts (type into a search engine "life story prompts"). You will find ideas such as: What was your first job like? Tell about an especially special birthday or Christmas gift. Who was your favorite schoolteacher? Where did your family go for vacations? How much did your first home cost and what was it like? What is your favorite scripture and why?

I have also found it helpful to use handy index cards, notebooks, or digital devices for keeping notes for whenever an impression, thought, or story strikes my mind that can be developed later. Don't let a good idea get away! Compiling your personal history is an ideal project for your retirement years.

By the way, include not only stories. . . family jokes and humorous incidents can be fun to pass on through your personal history. Below are two examples from my life story:

We signed up our youngest daughter, Nancy, for speech therapy when she was about four because she didn't talk plainly. One day she came scurrying home from a therapy session and proudly announced, "My speech teacher says I have only one more yetter to yearn!")

* * * * * *

Due to our being away on a mission, a young grandson, Tanner, didn't meet us grandparents until he was two-years-old. He was instantly okay with me, but for some reason he was afraid of his grandpa. He wouldn't talk to him or even look at him. Then one day Tanner got up enough courage, at last, to acknowledge him, but he referred to him as "the daddy grandma."

Above all, writing and sharing your life story (and those of other family members) can be like serving a mission, wherein you teach and testify of the gospel of Jesus Christ to your family—even for generations to come.

Things to consider including in a life story:

- Faith journal, miracle journal, or gratitude journal
- A photo journal
- Favorite scriptures
- Gospel principles applied to life lessons

- Copy of talks you have given and lessons you have taught
- Favorite family recipes, and the stories behind them
- Patriarchal Blessings, or sections you feel would be appropriate to share
- Priesthood line of authority
- Stories
- Testimony

If you haven't already done so, I would encourage you to make this a record year by compiling your life story. You will be forever glad you did.

CHAPTER THIRTEEN

Serving In Many Ways

*P*lease bless Grandma and Grandpa on their mission," prayed three-year-old Robbie.

Robbie doesn't know much about missions, but he does know a lot about Grandma and Grandpa and that whatever they are doing must be important.

His mother remarked, "It's interesting that Grandma and Grandpa are even a stronger influence in our home in their absence due to missionary service than they were in their presence. While they are away we pray for them as a family in every prayer, we talk about them more frequently than usual, we look at their pictures with extra interest, and we know what they do all day long every day."

"Even the older children gather around when their letters arrive," she added. *"The word 'mission' commands a lot of respect in our home. Whatever a mission is, our children want to do it, too. Thank you, Grandma and Grandpa!"*

Being a good example and mission motivator is just one way a mission can bless our families—and you and me as grandparents. It adds a new and extra dimension to life, whether it be the proselyting or service kind, close to home or far away, or a short- or long-term assignment.

Missions have enriched my life immeasurably. They have provided treasure troves of memories. I continue to draw from what I learned and experienced in countless ways. They have given me everlasting friendships.

A mission brings about joy now and eternal blessings forever. This scripture explains how it happens:

"And now, if your joy will be great with one soul that you have brought unto me into the kingdom of my Father, how great will be your joy if you should bring many souls unto me!"

Doctrine and Covenants 18:16

Along with missions, there are many ways to serve. I remember well then-President Uchtdorf's general conference message in October 2008 when he admonished us to "lift where you stand." I thought that was a wonderful notion until the day came when "standing" became a problem for me. It occurred to me then, with respectful apologies to Elder Uchtdorf, that perhaps some of us could "lift" where we "sit." (You can lift from a bed, too.) There are many of us in our eighties and nineties who are better sitters than standers.

Some sitting service opportunities that are unique to members of The Church of Jesus Christ of Latter-day Saints come through family history and temple work.

Indexing is a very good way to serve as you grow older. Like numerous others, my friend Lia Davis has indexed thousands of names. This brings her a great deal of satisfaction as she contemplates how much of eternal significance is being accomplished. Lia shared the following with me:

"It was a long time ago while growing up in the Netherlands that a member of the Church in the United States worked on the genealogy of my father's line. After emigrating to America, my mother was then able to do the research herself.

"Now it is my turn to continue doing some genealogy work in the form of research while attending the temple for my ancestors: initiatory, endowments, and sealings. One of the things I especially have enjoyed is indexing in the perimeters of my own home, as few or as many names as time permitted.

"It has been rewarding to have several comments left on my website thanking me for the work I did so that further work could now progress on several lines because I had completed some information for them. What a blessing that has been! I am so very grateful I have been able to participate in genealogy and temple work, especially now as our prophet encourages us to do work which is needed for both the living and the dead."

Diane, my daughter, has prepared temple-ready cards by the hundreds, making it so we family members can do the proxy work for our own ancestors each time we attend the temple. This makes the experience especially meaningful.

Temple service is one of the most spiritually rewarding of any endeavor as it brings about blessings on both sides of the veil.

There are people who are bedridden or otherwise seriously handicapped who have found unique ways to do good and help others.

Thom Kearl, a member of a neighboring ward, amazes me and the many who know him with all the good he accomplishes from a recliner with only his computer and smart phone in hand.

He has given me permission to share his life-altering story. First, I want to say that Thom is an energetic, personable man, a devoted husband and father, a successful businessman, a world traveler, and a leader in the community and church. He was a beloved bishop of a young single adult ward. It seems that everyone knows and loves Thom.

He tells about being raised by a faithful, spiritually deep father and an insightful, wise mother, and about being guided by the Spirit as he grew up. In retrospect he can see how his life had prepared him, remarkably, for what was to come.

One day in 2021, COVID-19 struck him with such force that it changed him (and his wife, Nanette, and their family) forever.

The traumatic result was that Thom spent 223 days in the intensive care unit (ICU) plus 32 additional days in the rehabilitation unit at the Intermountain Medical Center near Salt Lake City. The hospital claims his was the longest ICU stay due to COVID ever reported by a hospital in the United States. He "died" five times, but he was successfully (and miraculously) resuscitated five times.

The windows of heaven were opened before him, and he was blessed with experiences so sacred that, I feel, only he can relate them.

Thom and Nanette Kearl at home

Thom spends time each day by reaching out through his emailing, texting, and phone calling and testifies to loved ones who have questions or who are struggling with their faith about what he learned on the other side of the veil. He feels like a latter-day Lazarus, feeding the sheep. His message is that the Book of Mormon is true; God is real; Jesus Christ, our Savior and Redeemer, lives; life is all about agency, love, and family."

Just as giving and serving are virtues, it is important to recognize that so is accepting and receiving. In fact, becoming a gracious receiver is integral to service. Every "giver" needs a "receiver."

It is a challenge for me to be a good receiver. Instead of my taking a covered dish to a neighbor, now the neighbor brings the covered dish to me. In place of accepting it with an apology, I am learning to respond with a sincere "thank you."

I value the "ministering" program of The Church of Jesus Christ of Latter-day Saints. It is the inspired way the Church looks after its own. It is a step toward becoming Christ-like.

The two ministering brothers from my ward, Paul and Dan, who look after me are thoughtful, attentive, and reliable. In addition to being available to assist me at any time from providing some tech support with my computer to moving a heavy box, they go the "second mile" by visiting monthly and leaving a message.

My ministering sisters, Ann and Naoma, can be more aptly described as ministering angels. They magnify the spirit of their callings with wisdom, insight, and love. Their visits are delightful, and they often bring garden produce, such as tomatoes or raspberries picked the very day, and muffins or cinnamon rolls from their oven right to my table. Even a favorite scripture quote in my mail slot brightens my day.

In an ideal situation, it is the family who is the first responder in case of need. I am very fortunate in that my situation is an ideal one: five of our eight children live within 30 minutes of me. In addition to Sunday dinners on a rotation basis at their homes, each one has a day of the week to contact or visit me and be responsible for anything I might need. The system is working well. That they are good to me is such an understatement of what they really do that I smile to myself each time I think or talk about it. Let me just say, they are there for me, in every way, at any time.

Wisely, my children have built some flexibility into this program so it can be adjusted as circumstances call for it. For instance, if someone is busy or out of town they can trade days, or a spouse or another family member can step in. The grandchildren are quick to help out.

So, service can be rendered while we stand or sit, even if it's in a wheelchair—even if we lie in bed. And we can be of service by graciously receiving.

There is yet another category, and that is "becoming," as the following story portrays:

One day, after several hours of fun at Liberty Park with our two youngest granddaughters, Anna and Lucy, they enthusiastically expressed appreciation to me for the good time. I explained to them that even though I took them to the park, it was Grandpa who had provided the money for the rides, lunch, treats, and bird show they had enjoyed.

Then, back home, I encouraged them to go into Grandpa's den, where he spent most of his time now that he was in his eighties and in failing health and thank him. Anna thought for a minute and then remarked, "I don't see how Grandpa could pay for these things. He doesn't do anything."

She was too young to appreciate and admire Grandpa for his strong work ethic and how well he had provided for his family.

As we age and grow less and less productive, we have the opportunity to gradually shift from *doing* to an even greater characteristic, that of *becoming.*

Sitting in his recliner, Grandpa wasn't doing much, but he had *become* the epitome of good cheer, gratitude and appreciation, thoughtfulness, kindness, and faith in the Lord, Jesus Christ. During the last few months of his life, he actually glowed with goodness.

In his October 2000 General Conference address, Elder Dallin H. Oaks spoke to the topic: "The Challenge to Become." He said:

> "In contrast to the institutions of the world, which is to know something, the gospel of Jesus Christ challenges us to become something. . . . From scriptural teachings . . . we conclude that the Final Judgment is not just an evaluation of a sum total of good and evil acts—what we have done. It is an acknowledgment of the final effect of our acts and thoughts—what we have become. It is not enough for anyone just to go through the motions. The commandments, ordinances, and covenants of the gospel are not a list of deposits required to be made in some heavenly account. The gospel of Jesus Christ is a plan that shows

us how to become what our Heavenly Father desires us to become."

Years ago, following a weekly meeting of Primary General Board members, several of us lingered around the table to visit. We were discussing the responsibilities and assignments we had just received from our presidency when one of the women noted that it will be a sad day for each of us when we age to the point that we become useless in the Church. Someone else added, "Oh, oh. Then we'll be 'put out to pasture,' as the saying goes."

We were sighing and shaking our heads when Virginia Pearce got our attention by boldly declaring, "I will *never* let that happen to me."

"How can you be so sure?" we wondered aloud.

"Because" Virginia smiled as she announced, "I'm going to be a 'Christian-at-Large' instead."

A perfect solution! We all decided that we would become Christians-at-Large.

Fundamental to living the gospel of Jesus Christ is to try to be like the Savior by being unconditionally loving, kind, helpful, and of service to others. The scriptures refer to this as "charity," the pure love of Christ. Of all virtues, it is the greatest.

The Bible Dictionary defines charity as "the highest, noblest, strongest kind of love, not merely affection; it is the pure love of Christ."

It is this love that will exalt each of us one day. It is the love that we can continue to cultivate as we serve in our unique and simple ways.

* * * * * * * * * * * *

I don't want to drive up to the pearly gates in a shiny sports car, wearing beautifully tailored clothes, my hair expertly coiffed, and with long, perfectly manicured fingernails.

I want to drive up on a station wagon that has mud on the wheels from taking kids to Scout camp.

I want to be there with a smudge of peanut butter on my shirt from making sandwiches for a sick neighbor's children.

I want to be there with a little dirt under my fingernails from helping weed someone's garden.

I want to be there with children's sticky kisses on my cheeks and the tears from a friend on my shoulder.

I want the Lord to know I was really here and that I really lived.

--Marjorie Pay Hinckley

CHAPTER FOURTEEN

Resolving Our Regrets

In January of 1958, I gave birth to very premature twin baby girls, born at 28 weeks' gestation. Hank and I were surprised (shocked, actually) to have two babies arrive; we had expected only one and not until March.

Following the doctor's counsel, due to their extremely fragile condition, they were named and blessed by their father and grandfather immediately upon reaching the nursery. The "on the spot" chosen names were Janet and Jean.

Jean survived and thrived. Janet, the firstborn and weighing just two pounds and a few ounces, passed away at six days of age. She was so small we buried her in a doll dress.

Our family and a few close friends gathered for a brief funeral service. A pair of tiny booties was placed in my hand by the mortician who explained, "We saved these for you to put on your baby's feet."

But I couldn't do it. I was too weak from the toxemia and birth complications, too worried about also losing the other baby, and too teary to see well. I was completely overcome and overwhelmed by the situation. I don't recall where Hank was at the moment, but my sister Donette stepped forward and placed the teeny booties on baby Janet's teeny feet.

I have wished ever since that I had done it myself. Even now, 65 years later, I feel sad and tears well up in my eyes as I think about it.

Each one of us has regrets about things in our lives. As imperfect, mortal beings living in a fallen world, we all have missed opportunities, offended or disappointed others, failed to keep promises, broken relationships, made mistakes from tender to tragic, or have not lived the life we had hoped to live.

Instead of being tormented with regret and remorse, I think this little quote can provide some consolation and hope:

"She could never go back and make some of the details pretty, all she could do was move forward and make the whole beautiful."

Terri St. Cloud

It is easy for us "oldies" to ruminate on regrets, especially now as we have more time to reflect on our lives, but that does nothing to change the past and only serves to drag us down in the present. I think Satan uses regret to keep us from progressing,

Personally, I frequently engage in a simple bedtime routine that blesses my life. As I review my day, I evaluate it as to "I'm glad I did. . ." and "I wish I had. . ."

This forms part of my evening prayer and sets a tone of peace and rest for my night—and beyond.

Before I continue writing, let me interject a sweet 'I'm glad I did" story to the "I wish I had" experience with the booties at our baby Janet's funeral. I've noted with amazement— and gratitude—that often in my life an "I'm glad I did" situation mercifully accompanies or follows the regrettable "I wish I had" incident, thus providing an opportunity for me to repent of and apologize for anything that I am sorry I said or did or to be consoled by a positive experience.

In this case, it was the music Hank and I selected for the funeral that made me feel glad. My mother suggested it as she helped us plan the program.

She told of an especially beautiful, new children's song that had been introduced at a Primary General Conference of the Church in October 1957, three months prior, and offered to contact the nine-year-old girl who had sung it in the Tabernacle about repeating it for us. The young girl was willing to do so with her mother as piano accompanist.

Little did we know then that this new song, "I Am a Child of God," would become one of the most beloved and frequently sung of any hymn (in dozens of languages) throughout the entire Church.

That precious little hymn is all we have to remember Janet, but it is enough for now. I am so very glad we did it.

The adversary has another method as well that can stunt or even destroy our progress if we allow it. That is to harbor hurt feelings from the words or actions toward us by others.

There is a solution to all these challenges for me and that is to allow the Atonement of Jesus Christ to work in my life. The older I become, the more I recognize the need for the Savior's Atonement, how it can bless me every day, and how I should prepare to receive it.

This happens best for me when I humble myself and repent, pray and fast, study and worship, and partake of the sacrament mindfully. Doing this helps me to create a personal mode of "seeking and finding in all patience and faith." Then I "stand all amazed" as answers, comfort, healing, and peace grace my life.

My soul is stirred overall twice each year in April and October as I listen to the messages of General Conference. Specific talks give me, in a striking manner, the answers I seek.

A talk in April 2022 by Sister Amy Wright of the Primary General Presidency on "regrets" brought a sense of reinforced comfort to me.

> We all have something in our lives that is broken, that needs to be mended, fixed, or healed. As we turn to the Savior, as we align our hearts and minds with Him, as we repent, He comes to us "with healing in his wings," puts His arms lovingly around us, and says, "It's OK. You are only five—or 16, 23, 48, 64,

91. We can fix this together!" ("Christ Heals That Which Is Broken," *General Conference*, April 2022)

During General Conference six months later, President Russell M. Nelson offered us words to live by through urging us to "let God prevail" in our lives ("Let God Prevail," General Conference, October 2022).

I find that as I turn my regrets over to Him, and ask for forgiveness, I experience healing.

The enabling power of the Savior's Atonement also helps me to forgive those who have hurt me and to feel at peace. Perhaps the hardest person to forgive is me, myself, but even that is possible as I put my trust in Jesus Christ.

Not only does this do wonders in solving our regrets, but President Nelson also extended the scope of the peace and joy that will be ours to all facets of our life by urging us in the April 2023 General Conference to be true disciples of Christ. We do that through being peacemakers with charity as the antidote and Christ as the answer.

With faith that the Savior will heal all that is broken in my life, I can become free of regret for anything I did and from any pain caused by the action of others. I can then use my energy to be an influence for good and to find abiding peace and joy in my life.

CHAPTER FIFTEEN

Aspiring To Be An Eternal Family

Grandfathers and grandmothers like you and me pray for our grandchildren and great-grandchildren daily, even individually by name. We desire with all our hearts that our Father in Heaven's choicest blessings, temporally and spiritually, will be theirs. Then we set about with love and attention, faith, patience, and prayer to help those blessings come true.

A favorite scripture expresses exactly how I feel. I am sure countless grandparents are in accord with it as well. It is:

> ## "I have no greater joy than to hear that my children walk in truth."
>
> 3 John 1:4

The grandparenting "to do" list on their behalf can be endless but allow me to recommend just three ways by which we, as grandparents, can categorize our influence as we support our grandchildren and great-grandchildren in their mortal journey. We'll call them the "Three Es."

One is to be a good *example* in every possible way; the second is to *emphasize* what matters most; and the third is to *encourage* them in their efforts to love and serve the Lord. Grandfathers and grandmothers can be good at doing all three.

EXAMPLE

We all have heard the truism that there are three ways to teach a child. The first is by example, the second is by example, and the third is by example.

May I offer a story from our welfare/humanitarian mission in Asia to illustrate the power of example. It is as follows:

A Spider as Big as My Hand

One of the senior missionary sisters related a frightening experience to me that she had early in her mission while teaching English at a school in Thailand. She was in the restroom and came practically "face to face" with a big, black, fuzzy spider—as big as her hand—on the wall between her and the door. She panicked at the sight of it and felt she needed to run for her life, but there was no place to go except past the spider. She suddenly felt an overwhelming awareness of her grandchildren's prayers back in the USA as they implored the Lord for their grandmother's "courage, strength, and protection on her mission."

The terrifying creature never moved from its spot on the wall as she cautiously left the room.

In her next letter home, she related the incident to her grandchildren and expressed gratitude once again for their prayers on her behalf. A five-year-old granddaughter responded by saying, "When I grow up and go on a mission, I'm going to pray to Heavenly Father, so I won't be afraid of spiders."

The missionary gave thanks for being able to be an example to a grandchild about prayer and creating a desire in her to go on a mission someday.

There are countless ways by which we grandparents can be striking examples through our attributes, skills, and actions, even when we are hundreds of miles apart.

Living our life as an example to our grandchildren is best exemplified by our adherence to the First and Second Great Commandments. You know them well, but it's good to refresh them by rereading them as printed below:

> "Thou shalt love the Lord thy God with all thy heart, and with all thy soul, and with all thy mind. This is the first and great commandment. And the second is like unto it, thou shalt love thy neighbor as thyself. On these two commandments hang all the law and the prophets" (Matthew 22:37–40).

EMPHASIZE

Be careful what you emphasize as grandparents to your grandchildren because that is very likely what you will get. Children are extremely perceptive in picking up the emphasis or priority of our lifestyles, however subtle it may be. Let's think for a moment and be honest with ourselves—how do we stress such things as grades, athletics, sports, music, games, new clothes, vacations, travel, careers, good food, fun times, cars, boats, cabins, and money?

All these things can be important, but are they all-important? Consulting the word of God in the scriptures clarifies the priority. We read it in Matthew 6:33:

"Seek ye first the kingdom of God and his righteousness; and all these things shall be added unto you."

The list of ideas of ways to place emphasis by showing love and spending time together, either in person or virtually, is lengthy, but here are a few suggestions:

- Be there in person or virtually for baptisms, ordinations, talks in Church, and so forth.

- Talk and work together.

- Play together.

- Read and study together (scriptures, *Come Follow Me* manual, *For the Strength of Youth* booklet).

- Attend their family home evening, personally or virtually.

- Help them arrange to do vicarious baptisms in a temple.

- Sing and play musical instruments together.

- Develop talents and share hobbies with one another.

- Teach and testify with them.

- Worship together.

- Pray together.

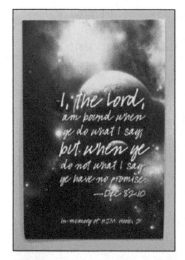

Quilt border: "Choose ye this day whom ye will serve. But as for me and my house, we will serve the Lord." Joshua 24:15

Be prepared to remind them in various ways what matters most. For instance, family mission statements or family mottos can be posted. (See above for examples.)

ENCOURAGE

"Grandma always believed in me," spoke our daughter Nancy in her sacrament meeting talk as she prepared to depart for her mission.

Grandparents have a unique relationship with their grandchildren, so they love differently from parents. Grandparents have a perspective and wisdom that can only be earned after years of learning and experiencing, thereby coming to understand life better through the bigger picture.

I keep notes on my calendar about the various activities and accomplishments of my grandchildren and now great-grandchildren. This way I can call, text, or send a note to show love, extend congratulations for birthdays or other special occasions, or uplift them. Most important, I can make certain that the occasions of everlasting significance receive the attention they merit.

Here are some ways to encourage your grandchildren:

- Talk and listen to them.
- Take pictures.
- Write letters, send texts, mail cards, and make phone calls.
- Visit them.
- Share your testimony and love of the gospel with them on a personal level.
- Coach them in endeavors such as reading the Book of Mormon, keeping a journal, attending seminary, and accepting a calling in their ward.

- Show interest as they prepare for baptism or to receive the priesthood.

- Be their number one cheerleader; head up their "fan club" in worthy pursuits.

- Go places together such as Church museums and historical sites, and temples.

There is a way by which much of the above can be accomplished and that is through family traditions.

Activities, repeated over and over again, become the stories that families write together. They develop into traditions.

Traditions can be as simple as telling stories and playing games; traditions can be as consistent as eating Sunday dinners; and traditions can be as involved as vacationing and traveling together.

Traditions can be about things we eat, such as foods from favorite recipes. We have five-star cooks in our family and collecting and sharing gourmet recipes has become an indoor sport, but there is one "dish" we prepare that is simple to make and far from being fancy and that shows up at almost *every* activity by popular demand. In fact, we could hardly have a party without it. It is Special K Bars.

An added meaning to Special K Bars is to use a heart-shaped cookie cutter to cut pieces for serving.

Special K Bars

Base:

1 cup sugar

1 cup light Karo Syrup

1 cup peanut butter

6 heaping cups Special K Cereal

In saucepan, add sugar and light Karo Syrup and bring to a boil.

Remove from heat and add the peanut butter and stir until combined.

Mix in the Special K Cereal and press into buttered 9x11 dish.

Topping:

8 oz. chocolate chips

8 oz. butterscotch chips

Melt chocolate and butterscotch chips together and spread on top of base. When cool, cut into squares and serve.

Traditions can be both enjoyable and serious. In other words, they can be entertaining, educational, and spiritual, or a creative blend of each.

Fun family traditions are often centered around birthdays, holidays, and other special occasions.

At our house, we always sing, "Happy Birthday" in Dutch whenever we gather for a party. Even in-laws joining the family are good sports and do their best to get their tongues around "Lang Zal Hij Leven" (Long Shall He Live).

We also perpetuate another popular connection to our Dutch heritage by celebrating "Sint Nicolaas Dag" (December 6). We place wooden shoes near the children's bedroom doors while they are sleeping so the children wake up to a treat from St. Nicholas such as a piece of chocolate candy, a small gift, and/or a piece of fruit such as an orange.

Traditions can be related to such milestones as baby births and blessings, baptisms, ordinations, mission calls, graduations, marriages, and funerals.

They can be prepared for and focused on united fasting and prayer when there is physical or mental illness in the family. This can also take place when someone has a particular need, such as a life-altering decision to make, a job to secure, an examination to pass, or some type of require-ment or performance of major challenge.

Traditions can bring about laughter or tears; they can draw us nearer to the covenant path.

Traditions bring about solid roots to the past; traditions provide rich, deep, meaningful happenings in the present; traditions offer hope and joy for the future.

In homes where the gospel of Jesus Christ is clearly taught by example, emphasized above everything else, and living it is highly encouraged, children are more likely to under-stand why the gift of eternal life is the greatest of all the gifts of God (see Doctrine and Covenants 14:7).

Preparing them to be worthy of that gift is of the highest priority; doing so matters so much, in fact, that nothing else can compare. Nothing even comes close. In the words of an 18th century clergyman, often quoted by Elder Neal A. Maxwell, we are powerfully reminded:

"If you do not choose the kingdom of God first, it will in the end make no dif-ference what you have chosen instead."

–William Law

I am assured, as declared in Romans 8:28, that all things, including the joy of an eternal family, will work together for the good to them who love God.

Love & Legacy Packets

You may want to consider a way to share your testimony and have a faith-promoting, positive influence on your great-grandchildren who may be young or not yet born.

For example, I am leaving a written testimony and photo of both Hank and me for each living or potential great-grandchild. In addition, I am collecting a few keepsake things to be included in what we call our "Love and Legacy" packet.

This packet is just a large, plastic expandable envelope from an office supply store that contains such items as digitized copies of our life stories, Hank's conversion story, a synopsis of my book,

The Art of Homemaking, a white hand-
kerchief (plain for the boys, edged with
lace for the girls) and a picture of the
Salt Lake Temple.

Example of my Love & Legacy packets

CHAPTER SIXTEEN

Living In The Last Days

It is the twenty-first century. At the risk of over-simplification, it seems there are two prevailing conditions on earth in varying degrees and with various combinations during these last days before the Second Coming of the Savior. One consists of the love and light that exists among many people. The other is the hate and darkness that afflicts much of the world. Our wellbeing and happiness depend on which we embrace and cultivate.

The Savior Jesus Christ is the source of the love and light. Love and hate cannot co-exist, and light dispels darkness. The closer we draw to Jesus Christ and the more we follow Him the stronger will be the love and the brighter will be the light until the perfect day.

The gospel of Jesus Christ is being restored in its fulness through His church. There is a prophet in the land who is inviting us to follow him and thereby fill our lives with love and light.

The gospel is being declared through technology from rooftops like never before. Hundreds of temples dot the earth. Israel is being rapidly gathered on both sides of the veil. Faithful latter-day saints everywhere have made covenants and are keeping His commandments. Personal peace and inner joy bless our lives.

We rejoice when loved ones—our children and grandchildren—follow the prophet and worship Jesus Christ by keeping commandments and honoring covenants.

An extremely sad reality of these latter days is that a few of these loved ones, mine and perhaps yours, are turning away from the prophet and disregarding his pleas and invitations to seek love and light. They are distancing themselves from the Church, ignoring the commandments, and breaking their covenants or failing to make them in the first place.

It is such grief and heartbreak that this chapter is addressing.

Over the years, I have learned, although slowly, that worrying is counterproductive. Someone once said, "Worrying is like sitting in a rocking chair; it keeps you busy but it doesn't get you anywhere."

An early experience with such worry was mine as the mother of a teenager. I was consumed, in fact, with concern over our eldest son who was rebellious at times. I would lie awake at night, my mind racing with despairing thoughts about the tragic consequences he may be bringing upon himself. And then something happened that helped me learn that I could redirect that nervous energy and instead of worrying, use it to help find solutions.

I vividly recall attending a stake leadership meeting in about 1974 and being deeply moved as someone read to us the story of Alma fasting and praying for his wayward son. I had heard the story many times, but that evening, it wasn't Alma's son I was learning about, it was my son. Suddenly I knew that through fasting and prayer, our son would be saved. He was not progressing spiritually as we would hope and was making some wrong choices. Therefore, from the time he was 15 until he was nearly 19, I fasted for him one day a week and Hank attended the temple very early every Friday morning on his way to the office, keeping his name on the prayer roll.

Slowly but certainly changes began taking place. No heavenly angels ministered to him that I know of, but many earthly angels, including a wise bishop and good friends, came into his life and made a difference.

Miracles, mostly small ones, took place. A major miracle happened after dinner one evening when he was 17. He announced that he was going with a group of boys of questionable behavior to a town beyond the Utah border where drinking and gambling were the main attraction. I knew there was nothing good for him there. Hank wasn't home so I pleaded with him not to go. He pushed me aside and left the house. I ran to my room and cried in prayer to my Heavenly Father to protect my boy that night. Just as I rose from my knees, the front door opened and he came in and simply said, "I decided not to go."

That was the turning point. Things improved rapidly from then on. He attended church regularly, gained a testimony, served an honorable mission, married in the temple, and he and his wife raised five faithful children in their gospel-centered home. The children have moved on to bring about another generation born in the covenant and growing up in gospel-centered homes.

I am grateful beyond words to my Father in Heaven for how beautifully this story is turning out.

I am also deeply grateful for what the experience taught me about trusting the Lord through faith, prayer, and His word in the scriptures.

He declared, as recorded in our Pearl of Great Price,

> "For behold, this is my work and my glory—to bring to pass the immortality and eternal life of man."
>
> Moses 1:39

Saving His children is HIS work and glory, not mine. I can only help by exercising faith in Him and trying not to make things worse.

Heavenly Father loves each one of us beyond expression and fully understands our circumstances. He knows the challenges and trials of living in the last days. We can trust in his promises to us to save His children.

On my desk where I see it a dozen times a day is a small, framed copy of a revelation from the Lord to the Prophet Joseph Smith in the dark, dreary dungeon of the Liberty

Jail. It relates precisely to what I need to know and do in these words:

> "Therefore, dearly beloved brethren, let us cheerfully do all things that lie in our power; and then may we stand still, with the utmost assurance, to see the salvation of God, and for His arm to be revealed."
>
> Doctrine and Covenants 123:17

So now, as the matriarch of an ever-expanding family I'm doing my best to implement this scripture in my life. Instead of worrying, I am trying to cheerfully do all that I can while I put my trust in the Lord. In short, I am endeavoring to live in such a manner that others, especially those who have wandered, know of my love for them and see the light of gospel living radiating from me.

Following is a list of things that I have learned I can do:

Show genuine love and acceptance

Although I don't agree with some of the choices a few of my loved ones make, I look for the good that is in them. They have lots of fine qualities and virtues. (It can be helpful to make a list of them for each person in mind.) I hope and pray that they will feel the love I have for them just because they are mine.

Speak words that edify, heal, comfort, encourage, and strengthen

I need to be careful that my words, even the tones of my voice, do not convey judgment. I pray for inspiration that what I say can uplift all those with whom I interact.

Allow loved ones to learn and grow from the trials of mortality

As a mother and grandmother, I am tempted to rush in and try to "fix" everything that goes wrong. But not only would I fail miserably in the attempt, I could thwart the ways of the Lord and the curriculum He has designed for each one of us. Learning from our own mistakes is often necessary for our growth and progress. It can also help us to trust Him as we strive to become more like Him. The trials of mortality are what bring us to know our Savior.

Stand firm and immovable on solid gospel ground

I believe I can be an influence for good in the lives of family members as I faithfully live the gospel and keep my covenants. Hopefully, the joy I find in living the gospel will be discernable to others as a light shining brightly and radiating to others.

Fast and pray, place names on the temple prayer roll, be active in temple service, and seek priesthood blessings

What a sacred privilege it is to be able to supplicate the Lord for His spirit, guidance and blessings and seek counsel and direction from ministering brothers and other ecclesiastical leaders

Engage professional help from those trained to help me and my family

I am profoundly grateful to the physicians, therapists, tutors, teachers, and other qualified people who have guarded, guided, and protected our family over the years.

Live with hope

We live in troubling times. As I try to place my focus on Jesus Christ, I am able to have hope for a wonderful future. As President Russell M. Nelson said,

> "Our Savior and Redeemer, Jesus Christ, will perform some of His mightiest works between now and when He comes again. We will see miraculous indications that God the Father and His Son, Jesus Christ, preside over this Church in majesty and

glory. But in coming days, it will not be possible to survive spiritually without the guiding, directing, comforting, and constant influence of the Holy Ghost." ("Revelation for the Church, Revelation for Our Lives" General Conference, April 2018).

Believe in miracles

"The most remarkable thing about miracles is that they happen." (Unknown)

I don't just believe in miracles, I expect them. I count on them. The more I look for them, the more I appreciate them and acknowledge them before the Lord, the more I see them. I record them in a journal. I keep most of them sacred, only sharing their story when I feel moved upon by the Spirit to do so.

Know that everything will work out in the end

As I have already mentioned, not everything can or will be resolved in mortality. Some things take more time. I look forward to the spirit world with hope.

There are some situations, that arise either with questions or issues or in loved one's lives, that cannot be resolved quickly, or perhaps not even on this earth. Many prayers are not answered immediately. Therefore,

I have figuratively carved out a little spot in my heart, which I term a "holding space." There I keep unresolved issues or all-consuming worries until there is clarity, understanding, repentance, forgiving, and healing.

Furthermore, "holding space" opens the way for me to love someone and maintain a positive relationship with them even though we disagree, and I am thereby able to still keep my covenants and be true to my faith.

May I repeat, as we **"cheerfully do all that is in our power,"** we will be able to survive the challenges and heartaches of the last days with the **"utmost assurance"** in the arm of God. He loves us and wants what is best for us. Our trial and challenges provide us the opportunity to come to know our Savior. As we exercise our faith in Jesus Christ, we can be an anchor and a source of love and light to our loved ones. **Then we trust in God to do the rest.**

CHAPTER SEVENTEEN

Walking The Covenant Path

What significance do the numbers 33, 6, and 12 have? Do they represent some type of relationship or connection? Do they mean anything to you? Why are they of interest and included in this book?

During the General Conference of The Church of Jesus Christ of Latter-day Saints held in April 2023, a total of 33 talks were given, 6 of them were on the same topic, and 12 of them referred to that topic.

What was the topic? "Walk the Covenant Path."

This gospel slogan was first expressed in public discourse by Elaine Cannon, eighth Young Women President,

1978-84. It has gradually grown in usage, becoming heavily accentuated in recent years by President Russell M. Nelson and other current leaders.

"Walk the Covenant Path" is the most recent slogan in a series of gospel slogans familiar to members of the Church. Like many of you, I clearly recall growing up with various gospel slogans such as:

ENTER THE STRAIT AND NARROW GATE

HOLD TO THE IRON ROD

CHOOSE THE RIGHT

LENGTHEN YOUR STRIDE

I have fond memories of each one of these. I particularly recall "Choose the Right" because many of us wore CTR rings and other jewelry to help us remember to make good choices and be obedient to gospel standards and values.

President Spencer W. Kimball encouraged us to "Lengthen our Stride." Such a slogan was the focus of countless lessons and talks in Sunday School and Primary, and at home we were taught to live by it. (I visited an assisted living center once where above the mantle in the common room was a large banner that read: "Lengthen Your Shuffle")

Now we are hearing about the covenant path from every pulpit. It is included in numerous lessons and referred to in daily prayers. It is a strong, compelling, comprehensive, all-inclusive call to total faithfulness before the Lord.

The covenant path leads us to the Celestial Kingdom through the pure waters of baptism and the holy altars of the temple.

In the course of the covenant path you receive all the ordinances and covenants pertaining to salvation and exaltation.

These words, "Walk the Covenant Path", thrill me through and through. I rejoice at the very thought of them. When I hear, read, or say this phrase, I frequently sense a surge of warmth throughout my body. I experience a sudden feeling of peace and goodness all over. It is most desirable, and I am grateful for an all-important, profound reminder of the course I should take in life: to be a covenant maker and a covenant keeper.

Elder Dale G. Renlund, in an ever-to-be quoted and re-membered speech at a BYU devotional titled "Lifelong Conversion," said in part:

> "The best way to become a lifelong convert [endur-ing to the end] is to engage with the doctrine of Christ. The doctrine of Christ—faith in the Savior and His Atonement, repentance, baptism, and re-ceiving the gift of the Holy Ghost—is not intended as a one-time event. We are invited to get on the covenant path, stay on the covenant path, and par-ticipate in the doctrine's specified elements.

> "We endure to the end by repeatedly and iterative-ly 'relying wholly upon' the doctrine and 'merits' of Christ. 'Repeatedly' means that we cycle through the elements in the doctrine of Christ throughout our lives. 'Iteratively' means that we change and im-prove with each cycle... as we cycle through the elements of the doctrine of Christ, we arrive at a higher plane each time. This ascent provides new vistas and perspectives and brings

A comparative sketch of the covenant path ascending a mountain

us closer to the Savior. And we eventually return to the presence of our Heavenly Father as an heir to all that He has." (BYU Speeches, September 14, 2021)

It is with Jesus Christ that we, you and I, have the covenant relationship, and it is only through Jesus Christ and completely through Jesus Christ and always through Jesus Christ that joy is ours.

CHAPTER EIGHTEEN

Receiving Blessings From Heaven

When I was six years old, my mother gave birth to my eagerly prayed for, long-awaited baby sister, Donette. While my mother was busy at home with the baby, my father took me on Saturday morning outings during the year of 1940.

One Saturday morning, we went on a hike with our destination the summit of Ensign Peak to the north of Salt Lake City. Climbing up this small, but significant little mountain, we passed a rattlesnake coiled in the dry undergrowth. Daddy assured me the snake was asleep and wouldn't bother us. I believed my father—I knew I could trust him—and

I didn't worry about the snake. But I still clearly remember the incident.

We sat on large rocks at the top of the peak while my father pointed to a panoramic view of the valley with the Great Salt Lake to our far west, the oil refinery right below us, the Salt Lake Temple downtown, Liberty Park (my favorite playground), and the University of Utah. Together we admired the magnificent Wasatch Mountain Range in the distant east as he called my attention to the mouth of Emigration Canyon. He told me how my ancestors had entered the valley through that mountain pass.

For the first time, I heard the stories in detail of great, great-grandparents who were converted to the gospel of Jesus Christ in their homelands of the Netherlands and England and immigrated to Utah to join the saints in Zion. Theirs was a saga of faith, courage, and sacrifice. As I listened to my father, a sense of heritage and legacy began to grow within me, and a very special feeling washed over me. (I realized later that it was the Spirit manifesting itself in my life.)

I determined in my young heart that I would always and forever be true to the faith, just like our pioneers had been.

It was a mountaintop experience.

My father and mother continued this legacy of faith and gospel living, laying a strong foundation for me and us siblings to base our lives on. I am grateful to them. Now, as I have entered my ninetieth year, I am able to look back at how richly my life has been blessed. Something that gives me particular joy is to reflect on the tender mercies and miracles that I have experienced.

Throughout my life, I have been blessed with countless tender mercies and many miracles. In fact, I think there must be an angel on high watching over me with a planner in hand, orchestrating my life. It works far better than it ever could with just me in charge. It is filled with amazing coincidences and noteworthy timing in countless situations— on a daily basis. I have even experienced the miracle of the loaves and fishes as Hank and I were able to serve root beer floats to 350 young single adults when we had supplies for only about 100. I have witnessed miracle healings. I have been blessed to have numerous prayers answered.

In fulfillment of a priesthood blessing, I received healing beyond my natural abilities when I had both of my knees replaced the same day and was able to walk without support and drive safely two-and-a-half weeks later because Hank needed me. After a couple of very sick days at home, he was hospitalized with pneumonia, and my being with him throughout the day was important to both of us.

Many miracles are too personal or too sacred to write about, but there is a fairly recent one I would like to share. It happened as follows:

One day, several years ago, my treasured 40-year-old, chiming grandfather clock stopped chiming. The clock continued to keep time, but the chiming failed.

Alone at home and widowed, I missed the sound. Global concerns were descending as the devastating, worldwide COVID-19 pandemic was being declared. Potentially millions of people could suffer. The future looked bleak, indeed.

The silence of my clock reminded me of the role the gigantic Big Ben clock had played 80 years earlier from the tower of Westminster Abbey in London, England during World War II. It soon became apparent that the sound of its chimes sustained the British during the terrifying bombing raids. It was so reassuring that it was even recorded and broadcast throughout the entire United Kingdom during the war years. As long as the clock chimed, there was hope.

With this memory in mind, I made a note to have my clock repaired as soon as the COVID-19 crisis passed.

Then early in the morning of March 18, 2020, a 5.7 magnitude earthquake rocked the Salt Lake Valley. It shook my house on the east side of Salt Lake City--and my clock chimed. It continued to do so four times each hour. I view this as a tender mercy; hearing the dependable chiming gives me hope.

General Conference of October 2008 brought us an unforgettable message from Elder Jeffrey R. Holland on "The Ministering of Angels," both heavenly and earthly. He taught us:

> "From the beginning down through the dispensations, God has used angels as His emissaries in conveying love and concern for His children. . . .
>
> Usually, such beings are not seen. Sometimes they are. But seen or unseen they are always near.
>
> I testify of angels, both the heavenly and mortal kind. In doing so I am testifying God never leaves us alone, never leaves us unaided in the challenges that we face" (Elder Jeffrey R. Holland, "The Ministering of Angels," General Conference, October 2008).

Our daughter Nancy is a living testimony of angels in our lives. At age 42 she was involved in a horrific car accident, where she was hit broadside by a drunk driver at freeway speed and was subsequently hospitalized 35 days, 16 of which were in an intensive care unit. She experienced a miraculous recovery. Nancy had previously been promised in her patriarchal blessing the following divine protection:

> "You can live every day of your life with the complete confidence that you have Heavenly Beings at your side at all times and in all situations."

Paintings in my home comfort me. One of them is a small print of "She Will Find What Is Lost" by Brian Kershisnik. I keep it in my study, in a place where I can look at it frequently. I sometimes look at it through teary eyes as I reflect on ministering angels in my life and my family.

Many of us can recall Elder David A. Bednar's comforting talk on "The Tender Mercies of the Lord," in the General Conference of April 2005. He said,

> "Through personal study, observation, pondering, and prayer, I believe I have come to better understand that the Lord's tender mercies are very personal and individualized blessings, strength, protection, assurance, guidance, loving kindnesses, consolation,

"She Will Find What is Lost" by Brian Kershisnik
(used with permission)

support, and spiritual gifts which we receive from and because of and through the Lord Jesus Christ. Truly, the Lord suits 'his mercies according to the conditions of the children of men,' (Doctrine and Covenants 46:15).

"The Savior instructed His Apostles that He would not leave them comfortless. Not only would He send 'another Comforter' (John 14:16), even the Holy Ghost, but the Savior said he would come to them (see John 14:18). Let me suggest that one of the ways whereby the Savior comes to each of us is through His abundant and tender mercies."

I experienced a tender manifestation of the powers of heaven as I attended a session of a RootsTech Convention at the Salt Palace in Salt Lake City in February of 2017. Between classes, my daughter Diane and I visited the various display booths in the huge exhibition hall.

In the "Pictures and Stories" booth sponsored by Tom and Alison Taylor who had published our life-story books several years previously, I saw copies of those books. There they were, standing next to each other, on the shelf. Hank had passed away in 2013, and I was deeply moved as I saw us "together" again. It was a sacred moment as I sensed a symbolic, side-by-side positioning of the books.

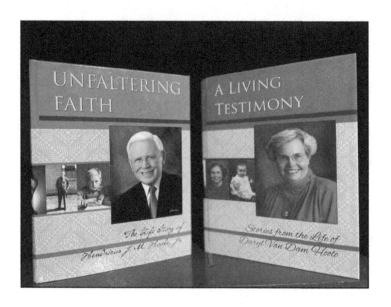

Hank and I are still side-by-side, figuratively speaking, as a parenting team, engaged in a labor of everlasting love for the exaltation of our precious posterity. A great deal of faith and work is being expended by me within the influence and strength of my earthly realm. I am assured of Hank's even greater power and effect from his heavenly realm.

Throughout my life, I have been the recipient of countless blessings from heaven. The blessings continue and I know that God is mindful of me and my family. Even though our family faces challenges, keeping these blessings in mind reassures me that I can trust in the Lord completely. Tender mercies are real. Miracles happen. Prayers are answered. God keeps His promises. Therefore I live my life joyfully.

Conclusion

These words from David B. Haight resonated deeply within me when he said:

> "Nothing touches the soul but leaves its impress, and thus, little by little, we are fashioned into the image of all we have seen and heard, known and meditated; and if we live with all that is fairest and purest and best, the love of it all will, in the end, become our life." (David B. Haight, "The Uttermost Part of the Earth," *Brigham Young University Speeches*, 1978).

Elder Haight eloquently describes the make-up of my life. It follows that it is also the sum of this book. Both the book and I are a product of the mostly idyllic environment that has surrounded me these ninety years.

The principles featured in this book's 18 chapters reflect this and bring them into sharp focus. Connected by the covenant path, from the first "Being of Good Cheer" to the last "Receiving Blessings from Heaven," they make up much of the art of aging joyfully.

You, a reader, have undoubtedly also been living by these principles because they are based upon true, eternal laws. God-given to his children on earth, you may have underscored them in your mind and heart and granted yourself an expression of gratitude that they were a highly significant part of your life. These principles reflect "the fairest and purest, and best" that has become you.

Even though the principles are timeless, the adaptations to daily living as outlined in the book are mine. Please allow the Spirit to guide and influence you in your personal and prayerful application of them with the hope that practicing them will be a blessing.

Through your reading, if you found any ideas or concepts or practices that were untried or new to you and you feel impressed to incorporate them into your life, I hope they will serve you well.

II | Conclusion

As members of The Church of Jesus Christ of Latter-day Saints, we have been blessed with the possibility of a glorious spiritual gift—an eternal perspective through our understanding of exaltation. Revealed truth made known to us through the Lord's Anointed promises us that life continues after this earth, that marriage is eternal, that families can be together forever, and thus the best is yet to come.

With this thrilling promise in mind, may I share one more story:

A few days before my husband Hank passed away in 2013, our three sons, Roger, Spencer, and Gregory, came together in our home to give him a priesthood blessing. Roger, the eldest, served as the voice. He spoke of some of the highlights of his father's remarkable life and expressed gratitude for the marvelous plan of salvation making immortality and eternal life possible. He spoke of the fact that Hank had been valiant in his testimony of Jesus Christ. I listened as my heart swelled and tears streamed down my face. I reflected with gratitude on the beautiful life Hank and I had shared together and the nine choice spirits sent to us and the grand posterity that would be ours in the next world. Then my heart nearly burst with joy when Roger promised him in the name of the Lord that "your blessings are just beginning."

To you, my dear reader, may a similar fulfillment of this thrilling promise also be yours. Through the holy covenants you have made, your blessings, as well, are just beginning.

Always remember that it is with Jesus Christ that you have this covenant relationship. And it is only through Jesus Christ and completely through Jesus Christ and always through Jesus Christ that joy is yours, not only as you age, but forever.

— Daryl

Acknowledgments

It has been said that two heads are better than one in making decisions or getting something accomplished. It follows that lots of heads, therefore, can be really helpful when undertaking a major project. I am thankful for the many heads—friends, family, and publishers—who have worked with me in wonderful ways and have fulfilled significant roles in making this book happen.

First of all, I appreciate my grandchildren, children, siblings, and friends who have asked, "How's the book going?" and have expressed interest and encouragement along the way. Often their comments were exactly the motivation

I needed at that moment to unlock the "writer's block" or feelings of being overwhelmed that had overcome me.

I am thankful to the "readers" who have kindly reviewed versions of the manuscript in its various stages, offering timely suggestions and pertinent ideas that further developed the text. Specifically, these helpful people are Becky Beck, Paul Henriod, Marijke Hoole, Ann Jackson, Dan Jones, and Kathy Stoker Kasteler.

My niece, Sharilyn Green, instantaneously caught my vision of the book as I told her about my plan to write again. She encouraged—even championed—my ideas every step of the way. She has been a fountain of excellent resource material coupled with wisdom and insights about living well in a complicated world. Her contributions have been invaluable.

I appreciate those who have graciously shared tender personal life experiences and thereby enriched the content, such as Jackie Gardner, Lia Davis, Thom Kearl, and my sister Donette Ockey.

A choice friend, Susan Goodfellow, generously drew from her years of education and experience as a professional editor and attended to every detail page by page, especially checking for inconsistencies or any other errors. A big thank you to Susan.

Patiently putting up with me and my tech inadequacies, my grandchildren have come running to the rescue every time I cried out in despair when I mixed up the "save" and "delete" buttons or committed some other "computer crime." There was no technological problem so challenging they couldn't solve it. Notably, they are Christian, Sam, Max, Jake, Landon, Brian, Tanner, Nate, Anna, and Lucy Hoole; Whitney Petersen; Abby, Andrew, and James Harris; and Aliza Wride.

Tech specialists among the grandchildren have dealt expertly with specific needs. For instance, Sarah Romney, a counter editor, checked and double-checked for correctness and rule-keeping in grammar and punctuation throughout the text. She has lived with me for a few weeks this summer, thus having "in house" tech support has been a boon to me.

Liesl Hoole, granddaughter-in-law and talented in creativity and design, spent hours—even days—with her baby Peter in one arm and her computer in the other formatting the contents, thus presenting the book's pleasing layout.

My special thanks to graphic artist and cover designer, Angie Panian. Her beautiful renderings of the swallow, a songbird and symbol of positivity and joy, have added the color and appeal to make this such an attractive book.

My granddaughter Emily Mecham built an outstanding website to reserve, in her words, "a parking spot for me on the internet." Multi-talented and creative, Emily serves me well. (www.darylhoole.com – hello@darylhoole.com)

Much credit is due to my children and their spouses for unbounded support, encouragement, and assistance. In addition to their countless services, everyone was willing to share family photos and stories and to perk up my memory whenever a prompt was needed. As a fan club, they've been "the best." They are Steve and Jean Harris, Roger and Sharon Hoole, Dan and Diane Romney, Mark and Elaine Quinn, Jeffrey and Rebecca Taylor, Nancy Taylor, Spencer and Ann Hoole, and Gregory and Kelly Hoole.

Three of them, Diane, Elaine, and Greg, have been "editors par excellence" as they have meticulously read and reread the manuscript, often weighing each word to say it just right. Thank you so very much to them for their good judgment and keen eyesight. There would be no book without them.

My eldest daughter Jean has been my over-all consultant, my assistant everything, and my do-it-all person—thanks to her with all my heart for allowing me to rely so heavily on her. Her contributions have been innumerable.

Joshua Boswell, the publisher, was one of our missionaries in the Netherlands from 1992-94 and has kept in touch since. Even though he lives out of state, he and his wife Margie visit often and update me on their outstanding family of 11 children. One of these visits was a year ago when he showed up exactly when I needed a publisher and marketer. He has been very helpful in contributing ideas on format and content as he took on the responsibility of publishing and promoting this book. Joshua is the founder of Copywriter Marketer which has trained over 35,000 freelance copywriters worldwide and Strahes Consulting whose clients include Sony, Google, St. Jude—and now me. It was my lucky day!

Yes—many heads have worked together with me to turn a ream of paper into a book. Each one has been indispensable to their task and a delight to work with.

They all join me in wishing you a friend who has taken the time and interest to read the book, the very best life can offer. Please know of our hopes for your aging joyfully.

About The Author

Daryl Van Dam Hoole was born in 1934 in Salt Lake City, Utah, the eldest of four children of Donovan and Ada Strong Van Dam. Growing up, she attended 18 different schools in various parts of the nation due to her father's military service during World War II. She also resided in the Netherlands for almost five years serving as a missionary and traveling extensively throughout Europe while her parents served as mission leaders.

She married Hendricus J. M. Hoole, and they were blessed with nine children. She is a faithful member of The Church of Jesus Christ of Latter-day Saints and has served three missions and held teaching and leadership positions on the ward, stake, and general levels.

Daryl has been well known for her book, *The Art of Homemaking*, and writing and speaking on home management and family living. She was a lecturer at BYU Education Week for forty years, except for two of the missions. She was awarded an honorary alumna designation by Brigham Young University in 2012.

Widowed in 2013, Daryl resides in their family home in Salt Lake City where she enjoys a large and growing posterity.

Made in the USA
Las Vegas, NV
17 November 2023

81036493R00105